DATE DUE	

Icarus World Issues Series

The People of This Place
Natural and Unnatural Habitats

Series Editors, Roger Rosen and Patra McSharry

THE ROSEN PUBLISHING GROUP, INC.
NEW YORK

Published in 1993 by The Rosen Publishing Group, Inc.
29 E. 21st Street, New York, NY 10010

"The Forest of the Spirits" was excerpted from the book *Mentawaï: La Forêt des Esprits* by Olivier Lelièvre, copyright © 1992 by ANAKO.

"Green Grass, Running Water" copyright © 1992 by Thomas King. Excerpted with permission from the book *Green Grass, Running Water*, to be published in March 1993 by Houghton Mifflin.

"He Tangi Ki Te Po" copyright © 1992 by Keri Hulme. Excerpted with permission from the book *Bait*, to be published by Viking Penguin.

"Iharang, the Healing Plant" copyright © 1992 by Inter Press Service. Excerpted with permission from the book *Story Earth*, to be published in April 1993 by Mercury House.

"The Masquerade Dancers of Havana" was adapted from the book *El Carnival de La Habana: Un Balet Afrocubano*, copyright © 1992 by Helio Orovio and Hector Delgado Pérez, to be published in spring 1993 by Editorial Limusa, Mexico.

"Passage to the Past" copyright © 1992 by Samuel G. Freedman. Excerpted with permission from the book *Upon This Rock: The Miracles of a Black Church*, to be published in February 1993 by HarperCollins US.

"The People of Forgotten Hills" was excerpted from the book *Yunnan–Guizhou: Couleurs Tribales* by Patrick Bernard, copyright © 1990 by ANAKO.

"They Took Away Our River" copyright © 1992 by Inter Press Service. Excerpted with permission from the book *Story Earth*, to be published in April 1993 by Mercury House.

First Edition

808.8
Peo

Library of Congress Cataloging-in Publication Data

The people of this place: natural and unnatural habitats. —1st ed.

    p. cm. — (Icarus world issues series)

Edited by Roger Rosen and Patra McSharry.

Includes bibliographical references and index.

ISBN 0-8239-1381-3 (hard). — I SBN 0-8239-1382-1 (pbk.)

    1. Developing countries—Literary collections. 2. Man—Influence of environment—Literary collections. I. McSharry, Patra. II. Rosen, Roger. III. Series.

PN6071.D46P46   1993   92-40928

808.8—dc20   CIP

                                 A

Manufactured in the United States of America

Contents

Introduction   v

Family Secrets   1
Fiction by Tiyambe Zeleza

The Great Ketchup-Salsa Debate   19
Nonfiction by Elisabeth Rozin

Iharang, the Healing Plant   29
Nonfiction by Dambutja Datarak with B. Wongar

Passage to the Past   43
Nonfiction by Samuel G. Freedman

He Tangi Ki Te Po   59
Fiction by Keri Hulme

The Word and the African Writer   71
Nonfiction by Jan Kees van de Werk

The Forest of the Spirits   85
Nonfiction by Olivier Lelièvre

Green Grass, Running Water   101
Fiction by Thomas King

The People of Forgotten Hills   115
Nonfiction by Patrick Bernard

Seven Days of Dancing: The Wodaabe of Niger   127
Nonfiction by Nijole Kudirka

They Took Away Our River   139
Nonfiction by Baher Kamal

The Masquerade Dancers of Havana   147
  Nonfiction by Helio Orovio and
  Hector Delgado Pérez

Glossary   161

Bibliography   163

Index   167

Introduction

If there were but one realm to choose from the many in which "civilized" man has most thoroughly revealed mindless cruelty and boorish incomprehension, it would have to be those places where his encounters with the so-called "primitive peoples" have taken place. Few areas can provide such a perfect setting for displays of bias in language, behavior, and thought.

The signifiers, at least as far as you and I are concerned, have tended to be those with the power to disseminate information on a mass scale. Books, after all, are written, edited, printed, and read by a population whose shared intellectual dress code is sufficiently similar to cause no scandal. To the Western mind, that which is scandalous—when it is not defanged by being "quaint"—is the totem image painted on a flattened piece of bark, the songs in the kiva, the elaborate designs of scarification; i.e., the evidence of an alternative history. And so when we signifiers find ourselves in "exotic" settings where "scandals" occur daily, as integrally related to the ebb and flow of life as drawing water, making fires, and cooking food, we have nowhere to hide. With every word, each jab into the air with a finger, the place from which we come is set against the foil of where we are.

These encounters between "civilized" and "primitive" mankind have been known to cause discomfort. The old colonials bared their teeth and attacked "heathenish ways" with a ferocity that seemed less to do with spiritual fervor than deep-seated fear. He who would root out one belief system in order to substitute another cannot afford an appreciation of nuance or tolerance. Injunctions that worked best and, of course, were most rigorously applied were those against going native.

We moderns have evolved somewhat, at least to the extent of having a postcolonial rhetoric that plays more appropriately to a broader audience. The fear of the primal, however, remains. The impulse to expunge a foreign taint, a primordial blight, a sense of shame, abides. Why do our confrontations with the "primitive" elicit these responses? Because no one, not even the colonial administrator of yore, can be so divorced from his essential humanity as not to see elements of Eden in certain states of nature. When the drum begins to speak to the back of our brain, and the dance to a repressed kinesthesia longing to be free, we remember the Garden and that scandal to end all scandals and all our woe.

"The People of this Place: Natural and Unnatural Habitats" speaks to the notion of the sacred grove, the campfire, the kampong, a pinpoint specificity of geography called home and the irrefutable logic of the ceremony and custom associated with being there. For this reason this volume of *Icarus* is devoted to those indigenous peoples who live in fear for their very survival, groups whose existence has been threatened by some profoundly scandalous behavior on the part of those who sometimes claim the highest levels of civility.

Roger Rosen, Editor

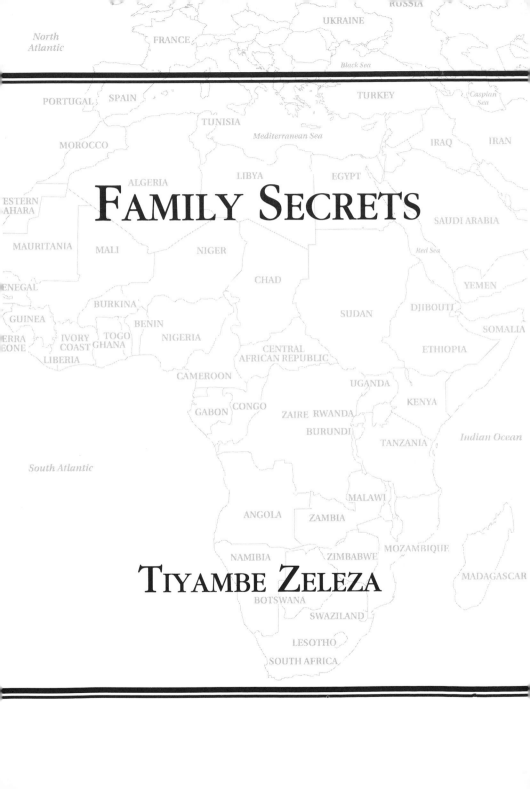

FAMILY SECRETS

TIYAMBE ZELEZA

T iyambe Zeleza was born in Harare, Zimbabwe, and grew up in Malawi. He received a master's degree at the University of London and a Ph.D. in history at Dalhousie University, Halifax, Nova Scotia. He has studied and taught at universities around the world.

Among Dr. Zeleza's honors and awards, he received the European Development Fund Award in 1977, the Killam Doctoral Fellowship 1979–1982, and a Rockefeller Foundation Fellowship in 1990.

Dr. Zeleza is the author of two works of fiction, *Night of Darkness and Other Stories* and *Smouldering Charcoal*. He has published several historical works, including *A Modern Economic History of Africa: The Nineteenth Century*, and *Labour, Unionization, and Women's Participation in Kenya*. He is coauthor of the four-volume *Themes in Kenyan and World History*. In addition, his articles have been published in Africa, Europe, and North America.

Dr. Zeleza is an associate professor of history at Trent University, Peterborough, Ontario. He lives in Peterborough with his wife, Pauline, and their daughter, Natasha.

It was a well-attended funeral. A celebrated event. Everybody who mattered was there, except the deceased's wife and children. Nobody was really surprised.

Dr. Bima was a renowned surgeon, probably the best in the country. He had a legendary reputation for taking on the most hopeless cases and pulling them back from the abyss of certain death. He was the chief surgeon at the National Central Hospital. He also operated a private clinic. Patients came to his clinic from all over the country and some even from neighboring countries.

His death came as a shock. It was front-page news. The reports said he had died of a heart attack in his sleep. He was only forty-eight. He left behind a wife and two children, but no will.

Problems started almost immediately after his death. His relatives, led by his brother and uncle, insisted on burying him at his ancestral home, beside his parents, as required by custom. Mrs. Bima had other ideas. She wanted her husband buried at the family farm on the outskirts of the city. And so the battle began. It was a long, ugly, and painful struggle, which captivated the whole nation for months.

Dr. and Mrs. Bima came from different parts of the country. They met as students and got married in the United States in the mid-1960s. When they came back, both their families disapproved of the marriage. Each family felt their son or daughter was marrying into an inferior community with strange customs. But the two persevered, ignored the ethnic predjudices of their relatives, and retreated into their own cosy little world in the capital city.

They both kept links to their respective home districts to a minimum. The city was their home, the place where they would retire, die, and be buried. Like many of their friends, they saw themselves as members of the new generation, born in the rural hinterlands but bred in the city. The new elite: young, educated, widely traveled, confident, wealthy. The leaders of the new Africa. Nation-builders, who had discarded the parochialism of traditional culture and ethnic solidarity.

And so instead of building a house in Dr. Bima's home village as custom demanded, they bought one in the city, a huge red-brick colonial mansion, from a European settler who was anxious to escape the feared chaos of independence. To their relatives, Dr. and Mrs. Bima were arrogant, lost souls, ashamed of their roots, blinded by ambition, greed, and individualism. Some years later they bought a farm on the outskirts of the city, far from both of their home districts. This provided further confirmation, if any was needed, that they had permanently forsaken the nurturing ties of kinship and tradition.

Dr. Bima quickly built a successful practice. There were many opportunities for young and enterprising professionals in the late 1960s and early 1970s; the economy was expanding and positions previously monopolized by settlers and expatriates were being localized. Everything seemed possible. The euphoria of having achieved independence, forcing the British imperial sun to set prematurely, was energizing. So successful was he that Mrs. Bima could quit her job as an accountant and concentrate on raising the family.

The family was late in starting. Many years passed before they had a child, although it was not from lack of trying. To their ever-observant relatives, this was one more indication that the Bimas were renouncing their African heritage, for children were the glue that held a marriage together and bound families, and through them the ancestors were reincarnated and seeds of the unborn laid.

Five years into their marriage, they had twins, a boy and a girl. Dr. Bima became more famous and prosperous.

When the children were grown, Mrs. Bima resumed her career as an accountant at her husband's clinic.

All that she had built with her husband was now under threat. His relatives insisted that, according to customary law, they had a right to decide how to distribute his property. Her claims to the family property rested on common law. The judicial system recognized both systems of law.

But there was more to the dispute between Mrs. Bima and her husband's relatives—led by his brother and uncle, who represented the clan—than the question of property inheritance. The clan wanted the burial to take place at Dr. Bima's ancestral home, according to tradition. Mrs. Bima insisted that her husband had expressly said he wanted to be buried on his farm.

And so before the question of property could even be discussed, Mrs. Bima and the clan fought over the question of where to bury the late doctor. Each side hired the best lawyers they could find. The courts were packed every day, and the media circulated riveting details of the trial, day after day, week after week, month after month. As the trial progressed, it became an absorbing contest between, depending on the observer, a lonely widow or a stubborn woman and her scheming or amiable in-laws, a struggle pitting against each other two ethnic groups, men and women, tradition and modernity, customary and common law, the old and the young.

To Mrs. Bima's lawyers the case was about the equality of women, their right to inherit family property, to make decisions about their lives and the lives of their children. Dr. Bima had not built his career and medical business alone, but with his wife. She was there from the beginning, sharing and shaping his dreams, successes and failures, the good days and the bad. Together they had created a family, produced children, the most enduring bond between two individuals, deeper than any ties of kinship, for children are the sacred fruits of a relationship freely chosen. She knew her husband's most intimate thoughts, certainly better than his relatives did, who saw him only on rare occasions. So if she said her husband had expressed the desire to be buried on his farm, the court had to go along. By accepting her opinion, her lawyers maintained, the court would be respecting the late doctor's wife and honoring his memory.

The prosecution maintained that the case was about the sanctity of tradition, and the need to uphold it, for without tradition society would drift aimlessly like a ship at sea without a compass. In the hurry to develop and modernize, society was avidly aping foreign ways and discarding values and customs that had endured for generations, sustaining people through the trials and tribulations of colonialism and giving them the strength to overthrow it. African society derived its vitality from its sense of community, its love and respect for people as members of social groups, rather than as alienated, atomized individuals. Marriage did not divorce one from one's community. The links remained powerful, primordial, unbreakable, as essential as the umbilical cord to the unborn child. These links had to be celebrated, especially at the critical moments of birth, marriage, and death. Dr. Bima's memory had to be honored by his people.

The defense called Mrs. Bima, an imposing, tall and beautiful woman, with a smooth, chocolate complexion, and bright eyes. She was always impeccably dressed in black. She stood her ground, firmly, courteously. Yes, she respected her husband, where he came from, what he had achieved. And she loved him, worked with him, and missed him dearly. That is why she could not countenance going against his wishes, allowing his body to be buried according to customs he had abandoned, letting herself be tormented by spending the night alone with his body in a hut and being violated in the name of chasing away evil spirits. No, she could not do that to him, yield herself to her eldest brother-in-law as his new wife. She had vowed to stay with her husband in sickness and in health, not with his brother after death.

The children, too, were called, two well-groomed and articulate young people who had recently returned from colleges abroad to attend their father's funeral. They corroborated their mother's story and wishes. Yes, their father had always talked of the family farm as his final resting place. They did not think they belonged to their father's "tribe," or their mother's. The whole country was theirs, the city their home. Tradition was not cast in stone, a dead object that could be stared at, admired, but not changed. Tradition lived. It was vibrant. It grew and changed with each generation. They were no less authentic, no less African because they did not live, behave, and believe like their forebears. They were the new Africans, the offspring of independence, embodiments of the dreams of nation-building and modernization.

Dr. Bima's brother and uncle shook their wise, bald heads, and their wrinkled faces trembled with anger and disbelief. They denied having any designs on their late relative's property. They had their own property, their own wives, their own families to look after. The brother was a clerk in the railway, and the uncle worked in a shoe factory. All they wanted was a decent burial for their esteemed brother and nephew. Dr. Bima had never renounced his ancestral home. Only recently he had expressed the desire to build a house there. Whenever there was a funeral he came and dutifully partook in the ceremonies. Before his departure for America, he had promised his parents that he would never forsake his culture like so many educated Africans, who returned from overseas with strange accents, manners, tastes, and sometimes wives.

Experts in cultural matters were summoned by the prosecution: learned men, endowed with chains of degrees, titles, and big words. The historians among them pontificated on the greatness of the African past and the need to revitalize it; the sociologists trumpeted the harmony of African societies threatened by imported individualism; the philosophers exalted the Africans' spiritual oneness with each other and with nature, and the interconnectedness of their past, present, and future; the linguists revealed that "home" differed from "house," that in cities people lived in houses, but homes could only be located on one's ancestral land; and the psychologists counseled that aping foreign cultures was at the root of the mental disorders that troubled increasing numbers of people, especially in the urban centers.

The trial lasted four months. Public interest never flagged. Mrs. Bima's supporters argued that the customs and rituals she was expected to follow were abhorrent. They had no place in modern society. The clan's supporters countered that she should have known that when she married him. It was the customs of Mrs. Bima's people that were abhorrent; they buried people no better than they buried dogs. The politicians could not resist getting involved, siding with Mrs. Bima or the clan depending on their ethnic origin, prejudices, and the shifting winds of public opinion.

All along, the body of Dr. Bima remained in the mortuary, almost forgotten. A few voices were raised that the trial was taking too long, that Dr. Bima deserved a decent burial, that both Mrs. Bima and the clan were pursuing narrow, selfish objectives.

The day of judgment was overcast and dreary. It rained heavily that afternoon, as if the dark, distant heavens had decided to wash away all the lies stalking the city and parading in the courtroom. Occasionally lightning blazed and thunder rumbled accross the skies, unmasking, for a fleeting moment, the face and wrath of God. The poorly drained roads were flooded and choked with traffic. Many of those who had intended to go to the court and hear the judgment were unable to do so.

The judges in their infinite wisdom decided to agree with the clan that the late Dr. Bima should be buried in his ancestral home. In the absence of a written will, tradition held sway, they proclaimed.

Some hailed the judgment; others called it a travesty of justice. Mrs. Bima vowed to appeal. Her supporters praised her courage, while her opponents thought she was possessed by the devil or gone mad. Some politicians suggested burial in the city cemetery as a compromise, but neither Mrs. Bima nor the clan would hear of that. Strangely, both parties were opposed to releasing the results of Dr. Bima's postmortem. That raised some eyebrows, including mine.

It was my publisher who urged me to pursue the case. It would make a good play, he said. I owed him one, he insisted, for I had not written anything in a long time. I was reluctant at first because I felt that there was nothing new I could add to the heartrending drama played out in the courtroom, day in, day out. But I needed the money.

I attended the appeal court every day, listening attentively to all the arguments, scrutinizing every gesture the lawyers and witnesses made, and watching the insatiable fascination of the faceless crowd that thronged the courtroom. In the evenings I pored over the arguments and studied the case. I was surprised to learn that what passed as customary law was codified by the British during the colonial era. It was no less a foreign imposition, an invented tradition, than the common law.

The case intrigued me. I had a hunch there was much beyond the theatrics in the courtroom and the screaming headlines in the papers. There had to be something else, the private story hidden beneath the public performance, the real anguish lurking behind the legal tussles. But the spark of inspiration eluded me.

A couple of weeks after the appeal hearings started, the judgment of the lower court was upheld. Mrs. Bima had no legal recourse now. Members of the clan were jubilant, everybody from that region was jubilant, and so were many politicians who had discovered a new theme for their rallies and speeches. They proclaimed the need to love, honor, and preserve traditions. The problems facing the country— poverty, violence, corruption, rapid population growth, and apathy—were all blamed on the breakdown of traditional values.

An angry Mrs. Bima told the press that this was a sad day for women and for interethnic marriages. But she would not be cowed, no force on earth would make her bow to the demands of her husband's clan. She and her children would not attend the funeral if the clan proceeded to hold on to her husband's so-called ancestral home. Instead, she would hold a memorial mass at the city cathedral. All those who truly respected her husband and believed in the power of love and the sanctity of marriage were welcome to attend.

So it was that two funeral ceremonies were held for Dr. Bima, five months after his death. The memorial mass was well attended, mostly by the more affluent people from Mrs. Bima's home region. It was a sedate gathering, a short and sad ceremony. The burial, held two days later at Dr. Bima's ancestral home, could not have been in greater contrast. It was a carnival. The body was flown in a chartered helicopter to the local sports stadium, where multitudes of people had been gathering for days. Anything remotely smacking of tra- ditional culture was on full display, from painted dancers and sacrificial animals to old medicine men and masked acrobats, who mingled freely with exultant politicians, ele- gantly dressed bureaucrats, children in bright school uni- forms, tired peasants, and gaunt old men and women, all of whom relished the temporary reprieve from their daily chores.

It was a reception befitting a great hero. The coffin was draped in the colors of the clan. All the region's luminar- ies—politicians, the clergy and businessmen, academics, athletes, and media personalities—spoke. It was an orgy of cultural affirmation, a celebration of their primeval oneness. Dr. Bima was glorified, his wife vilified, and his children forgiven. The absence of Mrs. Bima meant that not all aspects of the traditional burial ceremony could be conducted. He was buried the following day beside his parents.

The case was talked about for months longer. Academics wrote about its political, social, cultural, and even economic ramifications. My publisher kept pestering me on how I was coming along with the play. I lied that it was progressing well, but slowly. In fact, I had not even started writing it. I talked to people who knew the family, but they did not divulge any information that I thought was significant. Dr. Bima's drinking and womanizing were quite well known. I found out that his clinic secretly performed abortions, which was against the law. But all attempts to talk to Mrs. Bima failed. She refused to be interviewed.

Then one day I saw an ad in one of the local dailies. Mrs. Bima was selling the farm and the farmhouse. I told the publisher that this was my chance to get to talk to her. Could he open a temporary credit line for me at the bank so that I could make an offer? The publisher agreed. And so I approached the real estate agent selling the property on behalf of Mrs. Bima. I insisted on meeting her. She agreed.

I found her intimidating. She had piercing eyes that seemed to penetrate right through you.

"Where do you work?" she asked.

"I have just returned from overseas," I stammered. "I was a diplomat in Prague." I don't know why I thought of Prague, except that it was in some remote Eastern European country.

"Really? I know the ambassador there. He is a family friend," she stated matter-of-factly. I scratched my head and swallowed hard, hoping she would not pursue the subject.

11

She sat facing me across the room. It was a large sitting room, with a fireplace, expensive sofas, and wooden furniture, including a cabinet and bar made of fine mahogany. Framed paintings and family pictures hung on the walls, interspersed with hand carvings. The carpet and curtains were lush and thick. I felt uncomfortable, so I suggested that we talk outside as we inspected the farm. It was a sixty-acre farm. They kept a few dairy cattle and some chickens, and grew maize, vegetables, and some coffee. A small river ran through the farm, along which bananas and sugarcane were planted.

"My husband loved farming," she remarked.

"Why are you selling the farm, if I may ask?" I inquired.

"Well, I can't maintain it all by myself," she replied, and added with a sigh, "Besides, I need the money." She threw a quick glance at me to see my reaction. "Everybody thinks Lisani, my husband, left me a lot of money. He didn't. And the trial cost me a lot." She stopped and abruptly asked, "When would you like to close the deal?"

"As soon as possible. I have to wait for my wife," I lied. "She is abroad at the moment." She looked disappointed.

"I like the place," I reassured her. "I'm sure my wife will also like it."

We met a few times after that, ostensibly to discuss the deal further. She slowly opened up and eventually told me how her husband had died. They had always had problems, the usual marital problems, she said.

"I am told he was unfaithful," I said, trying to put it as delicately as possible.

"Yes, he was," she conceded forthrightly. "He started seeing other women soon after the twins were born. He tried to keep his affairs a secret, but I knew he was cheating on me. I said nothing, for I thought he would come to his senses and stop. But he never did. We lived a lie, both of us."

I looked startled.

"No, it's not what you think. I remained faithful, except once." She looked aside. "Why am I telling you all this?"

"You tell me."

"You are not interested in buying the house, are you? You want my story, not so?"

"What makes you think so? I do want the house; in fact, my wife is returning in a couple of days," I looked at her as earnestly as I could.

"You put up a good act," she chuckled. "I had you checked. You are a playwright, you have no money, and you are not married."

My whole body felt wobbly. I tried to apologize, but no words came out of my frozen mouth.

"I'm telling you because I want my side of the story to be known. Too many lies have been written about me. Let's start tomorrow."

"I'm sorry," I apologized. "I shouldn't have lied to you like that."

"I guess you wanted the story badly. Well, you'll get it. But on one condition. I have to approve it for publication. I reserve the right to take out anything I don't like. You can publish your full version only after I die. Agreed?" she looked at me with the sternness she had displayed in court. I nodded, reluctantly.

She started by telling me of the problems at the clinic. To maintain the fiction that I was a potential buyer, we met at the farm, where she would talk as we walked around.

"It all began when something went wrong with an abortion at the clinic. My husband did not perform the abortions himself. They were done by his assistants. Anyway, this poor girl bled to death." She paused. Her eyes became moist. But she swiftly collected herself.

I listened intently, making no comments or interruptions.

"The girl's parents threatened to sue us. It was not really our fault. She had come to our clinic when she was already

bleeding badly, after visiting some quack doctor. We tried
to explain this to the parents, but they were adamant.
They demanded money. We shouldn't have agreed. They
demanded more and more. I had told Lisani not to get
involved with abortions in the first place because they
were illegal, but he wouldn't listen."

This hung over their heads like an albatross, continued
Mrs. Bima, who allowed me to call her by her first name,
Madanga. They tried everything to extricate themselves.
They even toyed with the idea of hiring thugs to silence
the dead girl's parents forever.

"There was just one more straw that broke the back of
our marriage. One day I came back from work rather early
because I was not feeling too well. I was surprised to see
Lisani's car there, for he had told me he was going to the
National Central Hospital. Well, the bastard was fooling
around with the maid right on our bed!" Mrs. Bima's face
was contorted with disgust. She stopped walking and
inadvertently grabbed a maize cob and threw it away.

"That was it for me, the end. I couldn't take anymore. I
wanted to hurt him so badly, I cried," she resumed, her
voice choking with anger.

"He had abused me for many years. Nothing violent. It
was all psychological. He forced me to quit work after the
twins were born. After they started school, I insisted on
going back to work, but he refused, saying he made
enough for both of us. I kept pestering him. In the end he
agreed, but only if I worked at the clinic." She stopped
and turned toward me, giving me a long silent stare. I
avoided her eyes.

Then with anger welling up in her voice she resumed
speaking. "As I saw him on the bed with the maid all the
memories, the humiliation, flooded over me. I told him to
move out." Her arms gesticulated violently, as if thrusting
a dagger.

"Then I decided to drop the bombshell," she whispered,

with a faint, wicked smile. "Let's go in; it's getting chilly," she ordered.

We went in. But she was in no hurry to finish the story. She made some tea and put on some jazz.

"Do you like jazz?" she asked absent-mindedly, but not waiting for my response went into a long monologue on how jazz made her relax.

"It's getting late, you should be going. We will continue tomorrow," she said finally. She could see the agitated look on my face. She seemed to be enjoying it.

That night I could hardly sleep, wondering what was the bombshell she dropped on her husband and what it had to do with his death. I dreamt up all sorts of scenarios. Had she threatened to hire a killer? Or had she murdered him? Was that why she was opposed to revealing the results of the autopsy?

"You are early today," she observed as I came in. I mumbled something to the effect that I had a lot of work to do later in the day. She just smiled.

"Yes, where did we leave off yesterday?"

"The bombshell. You said you decided to drop the bombshell."

"Oh, yes, the bombshell." She stood up and went to pour herself a drink.

"Would you like some?" she asked.

"No, I don't drink this early in the day."

"Fine."

Before coming back to sit, she put on a jazz record.

"Where can I begin? Well, my husband and I were married for many years before we had children. We tried everything, timing, fertility drugs, all that stuff. He was a doctor, you know. But nothing worked. It turned out he was the one with the problem. A friend told me of a *sing'anga** who had helped them. Lisani was very reluctant to go, but I prevailed upon him. The *sing'anga* gave us some herbs and all that. A

---

sing'anga—traditional medical practitioner.

year later I became pregnant and the twins were born." She stopped. Our eyes met, and she nodded. Was that it?

"You don't understand, do you?" She could read my bewilderment.

"No, I don't."

"You men are slow. One time when he was away, I had slept with the gardener. That's how I conceived. As he scrounged for his pants and the maid jumped out the window, I told him the twins were not his."

The drink flipped from her hands and fell on the little drum that served as an end table.

"I'm sorry for the mess." She got up and brought a towel to clean the spill. I stared at her, unsure what to say.

"In the past, if a man was infertile, a 'hyena', usually the man's brother, was hired to do the job," she said defensively. I just nodded.

"Maybe I should make some tea; would you like a cup?" she asked, breaking the awkward silence.

"Yes, please, I would appreciate it," I said, although I would have preferred coffee.

She poured the tea and beckoned me to go sit on the verandah.

"I need fresh air," she declared. The verandah had a wonderful view. It overlooked a valley of picturesque beauty, with dense, green vegetation, rolling hills, and meandering rivers and streams snaking their way to a shimmering lake in the misty distance where flamingoes played.

"Well, he had a little surprise for me, too," she continued after we were comfortably seated. "He told me he had known about the twins all along."

The wicked smile and the anger were now completely gone from her face. They were replaced by a sad dejected look.

"After the twins were born, he took blood samples and had them checked. Their blood did not match his."

"'Why didn't you tell me all these years?' I asked him.

"'Why didn't *you* tell *me*?' he repeated. He thought I thought the children were his."

She sipped her tea slowly, almost as if caressing each drop with her tongue. For a moment there was silence, punctuated by the sound of birds singing, frogs croaking, and crickets jumping among the shrubs.

"Well, he moved into a hotel. We agreed not to let anyone know until we had thought everything through. A week later he was found dead."

"Did he commit suicide?" I interrupted.

"No, he died on top of a young woman." She shook her head, and tears streamed down her face.

I clumsily tried to hold her, but she gently pushed me away.

"You had better go now," she said, pulling herself together. She stretched out her hand, but her handshake was weak. I promised that I would not publish the story while she was still alive. She just nodded. My publisher has never forgiven me.

THE GREAT
KETCHUP-SALSA
DEBATE

ELISABETH ROZIN

© Seth Rozin

E lisabeth Rozin was born in New York City. She received a bachelor's degree at Hunter College and a master's degree in English literature at Brandeis University.

Ms. Rozin is the author of *The Flavor Principle Cookbook*, *Ethnic Cuisine*, and *Blue Corn and Chocolate*. Her work has appeared in the *Journal of Gastronomy*, *Natural History*, *Beauty and the Brain*, and *The Psychobiology of Human Food Selection*.

Ms. Rozin is a consultant to the food and restaurant industry. She also lectures on the history and significance of culinary traditions, emphasizing the fundamental importance of food as a cultural system, a constant tangible expression of how a society views itself.

Ms. Rozin is currently working on *The Primal Cheeseburger*, to be published in 1994 by Viking Penguin. She lives in Havertown, Pennsylvania.

What we eat is truly a large part of who we are. Our kitchens and our cuisines, our daily meals and our celebratory feasts, are tangible enactments of our cultural traditions: colored eggs and spring lamb for the season of resurrection, bitter herbs and unleavened bread for the Passover seder, turkey and pumpkin pie for the Thanksgiving feast. From our pots and pans, our griddles and woks, we experience from birth to death the sure knowledge of who we are, where we come from, where we belong. In eating, we not only take in the food itself with its nutrients, its odor and texture and flavor, but we internalize as well our participation in a family or a tribe or a nation, the larger social and cultural communities to which we all belong.

But the clear paradigm of "you are what you eat" becomes a bit muddied when applied to the American experience. For it must be obvious that as a people Americans do not share a single or simple set of traditions—indeed, America comprises and encompasses every race, ethnicity, and religion, a magnificent hodgepodge, the most varied human smorgasbord ever assembled on one soil. Is the United States merely a conglomeration of traditions, separate and individual, or do Americans participate, no matter what their background, in the larger something called "American"—and if so, what does it mean?

That question came to national attention in the spring of 1992 with the opening rounds of the Great Ketchup–Salsa Debate. The debate began with the announcement by the food industry that for the first time salsa sales in the United States had exceeded ketchup sales—to the tune of $40 million dollars.

If there is a single food that characterizes American taste, no matter how varied the Americans who consume it, surely that food is ketchup. Americans use it on every-thing from Big Macs to french fries to cheese steaks; it embellishes the breakfast fried eggs, the dinner meatloaf, and all manner of snacks and munches in between. We had a President who poured it on cottage cheese and a whole generation of children who grew up thinking Italian food was spaghetti with ketchup on it. The American GI is famous for dousing all his food with it, thereby turning any unfamiliar or suspect rations into edible food. Wherever we find ourselves in the vast American landscape, or, for that matter, throughout the world, the ketchup bottle is there, familiar, reassuring, comforting.

But when money talks, people listen; the salsa sales fig-ures raised issues and questions that had not previously seemed to be of any great concern. Was the long familiar ethnic balance of the nation shifting? What changes were occurring in the tastebuds of the mainstream palate? If commercial condiments are indeed a fundamental part of what America eats, what does a rapidly growing prefer-ence for salsa over ketchup tells us about who we are, who we were, and who we are becoming? Perhaps these ques-tions were raised because the sauces are perceived as being very dissimilar; but the fact is, of course, that both ketchup and salsa are made primarily of tomatoes. And when one considers that the tomato is itself indigenous to the Americas, the question of whether ketchup or salsa is the more "American" takes on a new significance.

The first European to encounter the tomato was the Spanish conquistador Hernán Cortés on his first voyage to Mexico in 1519. On the trek from the sea at Vera Cruz to the highlands of Tenochtitlán, capital of the Aztec empire, a priest named Bernal Diaz del Castillo reported of a local community: "So in return for our having come to treat them like brothers and to tell them what our Lord God and the King have ordained, they wished to kill us and eat our flesh, and had already prepared the pots with salt and peppers and tomatoes." That could well be our first description of salsa, for although the Spanish were later to add some new seasoning ingredients—onion, garlic, coriander leaf—the basic salsa consists quite simply of chopped tomatoes, salt, and chile peppers, those pungent little delights that were another unique food of the New World.

Salsa, in other words, was in the Americas from the start, a condiment or sauce eaten by native peoples long before the Spanish, with the rest of Europe at their heels, bumped into this great New World with its bounty of plants and animals. If salsa was thought of by native Mexicans as an appropriate way to spice up the flesh of offensive conquistadors, it was undoubtedly also used then as it is today: to add zest and piquancy to the daily diet of ordinary people, a diet based largely on beans and corn in the form of the unleavened bread the Spanish called tortillas. It is a meal that is widely consumed in Mexico today, and even where new foods have been introduced, the ancient combination of tortillas, beans, and spicy salsa remains an entrenched favorite.

If Americans, as well as the rest of the world, regard the United States as a nation of ketchup lovers, it may come as a surprise that ketchup does not have a long history on these shores. It was introduced to North America by English settlers, but not in the form of the bright red, sweetened sauce we know today. Ketchups, a general class of condimental sauces, had developed in England in the 17th and 18th centuries as a result of British contact with the East Indies—Malaysia and Singapore. The word "ketchup" was derived from the Indonesian word for soy sauce, *kecap,* and denoted a viscous sweetened soy sauce used to season foods. The English brought the idea of *kecap* back with them and designed ketchups made not of soybeans but of widely available local ingredients—walnuts, grapes, mushrooms. These ketchups, sweet and slightly spicy, were used as condiments on cooked meats much as we use Worcestershire or steak sauce. When the English came to the New World, the ketchup concept traveled with them once again, this time to find a new and higher fulfillment with a prolific American fruit, the tomato.

As ketchup was to find its most popular form via the tomato, so did the tomato find its way to the North American table by way of ketchup, and that was a fairly late development. The tomato was thought to be poisonous because it belongs to a group of plants that includes the deadly nightshade; until well into the 19th century it was shunned by most Americans of West European ancestry— the English, the Dutch, the Germans, the French. Gradually, however, people began to realize that the tomato was not only safe to eat but was an easily grown, prolific, and versatile food. Further, it could be preserved for winter use, when no fresh vegetables were available, in an attractive and appealing sweet and spicy sauce—the already familiar ketchup tradition. In 1878 the Heinz Company produced the first commercial tomato ketchup (initially called "catsup"), and the rest, as they say, is history. Ketchup quickly captured the hearts and the palates of mainstream Americans; it became the most widely used sauce in the land, the best beloved, the King of Condiments—until, that is, the spring of 1992 when salsa moved in to seize the crown.

So we have, then, the two protagonists in the Great Ketchup–Salsa Debate, two tomato-based condimental sauces that are structurally very similar but worlds apart in their history, cultural traditions, and perceived ethnicity. In one corner is the old familiar favorite, ketchup— thick, sweet and slightly tangy, and long associated with the traditional American "meat-and-potatoes" diet: burgers and fries, hot dogs, steaks, chops, meatloaf, and eggs. Its ethnic origins in the exotic lands of Malaysia and Indonesia are long forgotten, its translation from the East

Indies through the English condiment sauces all but vanished in its triumphant apotheosis as the all-American sauce. But though the sauce may have had its ethnic beginnings elsewhere, the food it has traditionally complemented is Western European in its basic contours, heavy in animal foods, fats, and dairy products.

And there, in the other corner, is the contender, salsa—spicy, hot, savory rather than sweet. Its ancestral hearth is the New World, and specifically the kitchens of ancient Mexico. It entered North America after the Spanish conquest, brought by the Mexicans and Spaniards living in the Mexican territories that were later to become part of the Western and Southwestern United States—the lands of California, Texas, New Mexico, Arizona, and Nevada. Although salsa has from the beginning been a traditional part of Mexican and Southwestern cuisine, it is only fairly recently that foods of Spanish and Mexican origin have begun to be widely accepted by the American mainstream and to have an impact on Americans of other ethnic backgrounds.

So what do we make of all this? Clearly, the mainstream palate is changing, in part because the mainstream itself is changing, no longer the exclusive enclave of white American Protestants of Western European descent. That mainstream has been changing all along, of course, with the influx of immigrants from all parts of the globe. It was not so long ago that Italian cooking, with its robust tomato sauces, its pasta and garlic and salami and fragrant cheeses, was considered ethnic exotica, "foreign" food, while today it has established itself as an integral part of the American table. So too in the last twenty years have the cuisines of Southeast Asia, Africa, Spain, and Mexico entered the American experience; their savory sauces, rich with flavorful spices, fragrant herbs, and spicy chile peppers, now comandeer the tastebuds of many whose ancestors would have rejected them.

In addition, issues of good health and nutrition have a major impact on food habits. The medical community has become increasingly vocal about the risks of a diet heavy in red meat, animal fats, and dairy products. In a quest for better health, Americans have begun to equate good nutrition with ethnicity, to see spices and aromatics and hot peppers as beneficial, and to accept a wide variety of ethnic traditions with their greater reliance on grains, vegetables, and zesty sauces as nutritious and healthful.

So salsa, though it has been around for many long centuries, is perceived as the trendy young ethnic newcomer, fun on the tongue, and good for you too. Ketchup, because of its traditional association with "unhealthy" foods—and its load of two other medically suspect substances, salt and sugar—is viewed with some suspicion.

But suspicion is one thing, rejection quite another. While there may well be an increased appetite for salsa, there is no indication of a corresponding decrease in the desire for ketchup. And that illustrates a well-known fact of human nature: People may accept and enjoy new foods, but they are reluctant to give up the old established favorites. Ketchup is a fundamental part of the American table, not only for the old guard, but for immigrant newcomers as well, who celebrate their rites of passage into the American experience with burgers, fries, and—ketchup! It will hold up its red neck proudly and share the throne with salsa, but its unique place will not be usurped. Already there are signs that the two are accommodating to each other: Ketchups are becoming spicier as salsas are becoming sweeter, and that in the end is what the melting pot is all about.

But it is curious indeed, and perhaps not inappropriate in the quincentennial year of Columbus' arrival in America, that salsa, an indigenous American food, is finding a place in mainstream American culture, and that a nation fed and grown strong on all the cultures of the world is finally embracing the long overlooked and unique culinary contributions of its own shores.

Salsa on your fries? Ketchup on your nachos? A return to authentic traditions or the creation of new ones? The debate goes on, and we will all play a part in the outcome.

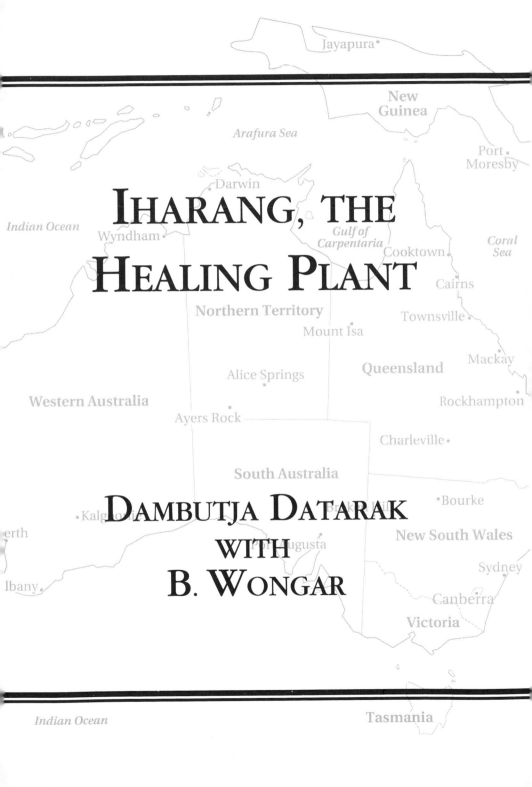

IHARANG, THE
HEALING PLANT

DAMBUTJA DATARAK
WITH
B. WONGAR

D ambutja Datarak was a medicine man of an Aboriginal people near Yirkala, in northeast Arnhemland, Australia. He died of the effects of radiation poisoning nine years ago. Before his death, he recounted the tragic story of his community to novelist and poet B. Wongar, himself a Serbian expatriate who emigrated to Australia in the 1960s and married into Datarak's people. Mr. Wongar's wife, too, died of radiation poisoning.

The following selection is Mr. Datarak's experience as told to and recorded by Mr. Wongar. It is excerpted from the forthcoming book *Story Earth*, edited by the Inter Press Service Third World News Agency, to be published in April 1993 by Mercury Press.

In the early 1970s a large mining complex mushroomed out of virgin bush at Gove Peninsula, Australia, a remote part of the Arnhem Aboriginal Land Reserve. No road connects Gove with the rest of Australia. The nearest town is Darwin, some 700 kilometers west across the tribal wilderness. The company, Nabalco Mining, imported their entire mining complex by air and sea. Several thousand white workers were also brought in. Before their arrival, there were only a handful of white missionaries in the area.

The arriving whites moved in by ship, airplane, helicopter. They blasted the bush, horrifying every tribal soul. Our people, the yuln, had lived in the Gove area for 2,000 generations and were self-sufficient and culturally independent—and nonaggressive.

Frequently scholars from all over the world visited the Gove region to learn about our tribal poetry, which dates back to the beginning of time, about our art and ritual life. Our elders—Mauwulan, Nanjin, Djawa, Djunmal, and others—were often portrayed in books and academic papers. Yet in the original agreement that leased tribal land at Gove to Nabalco for mining, there is no mention of our people and culture. The tribal healer, alone, had to care for both.

No day passes without my hearing my wife, Galei. She is out in the bush and howls, often at night. I wake up, listen to her calls, and wonder: Has she been caught in a steel trap?

I have known Galei all my life, perhaps even longer. Life stretches further back than the day a yuln is born. It does not end when he dies. In Wanga, my tribal country, every soul is reborn—you could turn into a tree, a bird, or a dingo, but that was before the balanda, the white man, came.

Why does Galei howl?

From the sacred site at Nandjaranga Cape our tribal bush stretches westward along the coast for many camps. The whites call it Arnhem Aboriginal Land Reserve or "black man's country." I was told there were more trees and dingoes out in the bush than the whites could count. Perhaps there are more tribal souls out there than drops in the monsoon rain. I used to talk about it with Galei; that was before she left me.

I first saw Galei when she was a toddler. A large tree had fallen on the camping ground, wounding her badly. They called in Mari, my uncle, for he was the marngit*. The old man grabbed his dilly bag and rushed to help, taking me with him. On the way I helped him gather dry grass and branches and made a fire to spread the smoke. He taught me that when going to help a wounded soul, people should pass through a smoke screen so that they do not bring flies with them. We even made a fire before approaching the camp to allow the smoke to saturate the bush and drive away the flies and bugs. Looking yellow, Galei quivered like the discarded tail of a lizard. She had a large bleeding wound on one of her hips.

Mari crushed bulbs of the white bush lily in a bailer shell and left them to soak. Before washing the wound with that, he gently removed the bits of wood and dirt, then he held the torn skin together. He placed mabanda leaves heated on the fire over the wound. Galei kept quivering, but did not cry. Maybe she was afraid or too weak to make a sound. The wound was then wrapped with strips of mabanda bark. The old man asked me to bring an armful of paper bark for Galei to lie on to keep warm.

---

*marngit—tribal healer.

Mari sang that night, as the healer often does, calling for the ancestors from Bralgu, our spirit world, to bring help. No ancestor answered, but a lone dingo howled from the bush: "She'll live." Mari told me that the dingo often passed on the news from our spirit ancestors to Wanga people. I was young then, learning the secrets of healing. The old man told me that when growing into a marngit one has to know not only the people but also waragan—dingoes, trees, and all other creatures: "We're the same mala*." I must have told Galei about it.

Lucky for Mari, at the time he was the tribal healer no balanda settled in Wanga. Now and then a steamer would sail around Nandjaranga Cape, bellowing smoke. That floating thing looked like a drifting log set on fire. Our people thought that the balanda were sailing on a raft and that they had set it on fire so they could boil their billy can** and make tea. Our women and children stayed away from the coast, fearing that the steamer might drift closer and bring the balanda. I often thought of asking Mari why some of our people have to run inland from balanda men, and thought he might tell me about it in time to come.

As far back as I can remember, the people said that Wanga had never had such a good healer as Mari since the Dreamtime, the mythical time. With him about, no yuln suffered very much from dislocated fingers, "running belly," or high fever. The right healing plants always grew in the bush. The people thought that he could even sing life into a tree struck by lightning.

Word about him must have spread far beyond Wanga. Missionary people living some camps away down the coast often sent out a message stick with some barley sugar, which meant that his help was badly needed. Galei and I both hoped that one day he might tell me why our people ran

---

*mala—crowd or clan.
**billy can—cooking pot.

into the bush when that steamer showed up around Nandjaranga Cape.

Mari often used to tell me that during the Dreamtime our Wanga was a plain of bare sand. Termite people lived then, eating trees, roots, everything. With so many of them about, the country ran out of food quickly, and they had to eat one another instead. Our spirit ancestors, who came from the sea at that time, separated the sand from the rocks and brought trees to the barren country. They made mangrove swamps, hills, rivers, and a large billabong* in the middle of the Wanga. Next to the billabong lay the ceremonial ground, Nongaru.

Before going to Bralgu, the ancestors passed on the secrets of rain to a yuln. Before the arrival of the monsoon, the men gather on Nongaru to sing for the clouds. Old Mari told me the clouds are lured from the far sea to Wanga by tribal girls brought to Nongaru for their initiation. Each of them has her skin smeared with malnar** and kangaroo fat. The girls rest in a grove of iharang bushes, waiting to enter the ceremonial ground and be broken by the tip of a boomerang to make them into women. Each of them is given iharang berry to taste. Pity Galei never tasted one. She would still be with me if she had.

Mari told me that those iharang bushes were planted by our spirit ancestors to help women stop bearing children. If Wanga women were allowed to breed like those ant people in the mythical time, the country could grow bare again. The ancestors left behind a pack of dingoes, who rest under a boulder near the grove and howl when the dark monsoon clouds roll onto the land. "No lightning ever strikes the iharang bush," Mari told me. That was before the balanda came to Wanga.

*   *   *

---

*billabong—cove.
**malnar—red ocher.

The first white man I saw in our country seemed mad about rocks.

He carried a small hammer, used to chip flakes from boulders and tuck them into his rucksack. That man gave Mari a metal darkgul* and a billy can;then he told us that both those things came from the rocks. Mari was promised that in time to come every yuln would receive the same gift. Old Mari had been given a metal darkgul by a missionary—Cross Man, we called him—who lived several camps away down the coast from Nandjaranga Cape. The new darkgul looked much sharper and shinier. Although the darkguls were different, the whites looked as much like each other as turtle eggs.

We call the white man Gunda, boulder. When Galei asked me how he happened to be in our country, I could not tell. I thought, however, that he might be a balanda spirit brought by the monsoon clouds. I had never met a man who would go round chipping boulders. He came just before our big ceremony at Nongaru. We had already made a pile of boomerangs, smeared them with malnar and kangaroo fat, each ready for the sacred ritual to make a girl into a woman. My Galei was to be initiated then.

Mari asked me to lead Gunda into the far part of our country, away from Nongaru, and keep him there chipping the boulders because no stranger has ever seen our initiation ceremony. If anyone intruded on Nongaru or the iharang grove, the dingoes would howl and our spears would hold him back.

Poor Galei, she missed the initiation gathering—she had to accompany me to the hills to make the campfire and gather bush tucker** for me and Gunda. Pity for her. If she had been initiated, she would not now be out in the bush, turned into a dingo and howling. I think she

---

*darkgul—hatchet.
**tucker—food.

reminds me that Wanga, most of it, has been taken by the whites. Our poor country.

When one of us dies, his spirit splits into two parts. One part stays in the country and turns into a tree, the other goes to Bralgu island for a while. The spirits return to the mainland now and then; turned into gnats, they hover in the air looking for a young woman who might be asking for them. A gnat appears in her dream first and then, if she nods, it enters her. However, no soul was able to be reborn in Wanga without a good family to grow up in and land on which to live.

That was how we lived when Mari was alive, and for many monsoons before that—ever since our spirit ancestors came here. Nandjaranga Cape, which juts out into the sea like a pointed finger, was created so that the spirits of the dead could go there to wait for our ferryman, Nangang, to take them by canoe to Bralgu.

This does not happen now; the cliffs of Nandjaranga Cape have been flattened and the place turned into a jetty. The whites built a pathway for some strong metal monster that looks like an immense serpent stretching across the country from Nongaru to Nandjaranga Cape. "Conveyor belt," Cross Man called the metal monster. The thing rattled day and night carrying rocks down to that jetty and pouring them into the bellies of huge ships. "The whole country could go that way," Cross Man warned me. Mari thought so too. Good that poor old Mari died some monsoons before. The day the old man went, he handed me the darkgul and billy can: "Take that to the balanda." He told me we have our own tools that we should hold on to.

Not long after the old man died, that missionary fellow Cross Man came to the bush looking for me. He told me Mari had appeared in his dreams asking that we do something to drive the mining people from Wanga: "Soon there might be no country left." Cross Man wanted me and other tribal fellows to go to balanda court in a faraway town and tell them what had happened to our land. He gave me a pair of shorts and a T-shirt and told me to smarten myself up: "Those people in town still think that you fellows are only part human." He told us we would make history: Never before had a yuln gone to white man's court to fight for his land. With new clothes on, we looked strange to one another, even funny. Our people laughed when they gathered to see us off.

No tribal healer should put on balanda clothes and leave his country at a time when it is in the grip of a curse. I thought that by going to town I might see Galei. Some monsoons ago when we were on that trip with Gunda, the white man took her away from me and fled the country. I have often seen her since then in my dreams, always ceremonially dressed. Pretty she looked, her skin smeared with malnar and wearing an armband made of cockatoo down and possum fur. Her fast-budding breasts were held by a harness to keep them firm. She looked ready to step out onto Nongaru and be made into a woman. Perhaps when coming to me in my dreams she is trying to remind me that no tribal girl should enter womanhood without being properly initiated.

On initiation ground the girls are seen by the spirits from Bralgu, who turn into gnats and hover in the air. They know to whom each of the girls is betrothed and what the country they are going to live in looks like—does it have plenty of trees, billabongs, yam, and fish? This determines how many children one is going to have—two, perhaps more if the country is vast and abundant with tucker.

The white man at the court called Judge wanted to know why we need iharang bush growing near Nongaru billabong: "The spirit ancestors wanted it that way." I spoke only our tribal language, but Cross Man was there to interpret every word I said. No other balanda knows our language. Judge wore some kind of headdress, made from the skin of a dingo by the look of it. He said he had heard all good things about what I did as the tribal healer and tried to smile: "Your people have been poor, struggling with stone axes since the Ice Age. Surely it would be unfair to deprive them of the benefits of the darkgul and billy can." He asked me if we had a "land title" given to us by our spirit ancestors—some piece of paper, I gather. Cross Man tried to explain that we neither write nor read. As for our ancestors, they lived in a mythical time when the rivers and mountains were made and the first yuln was born. "Is that according to our God or theirs?" Judge wanted to know.

On our behalf, Cross Man presented the court with a large bark painting done by a group of our fellows, showing our tribal lands, plentiful with yams and animals, many of which were sacred. In the center of the picture lay Nongaru and nearby iharang bushes gathered by dingoes; that was painted solely by me in red and yellow ocher— only the tribal healer is allowed to do it. Judge looked pleased: "It's a nice picture, I will see it is hung in my library." Judge wanted to hear from me about the darkgul and billy can given to Mari by the white man, and did he make good use of it? He even asked me if any of our people eat the rocks. Perhaps that white man Gunda said that we gave the country away for that rusting darkgul and can.

I asked at the court if they could let me see my Galei. Cross Man must have misinterpreted my request, for Judge looked at me: "Sorry, but this court cannot grant you a woman." They all laughed. Perhaps they thought I was asking for a white one. Galei returned to Wanga some monsoons later. She did not come to the bush to see me but went to her mala. It is further on from Nandjaranga Cape, along the coast. The sea there enters through a strait hardly a good voice long and then widens into a bay that would take a man many camps to walk around. One catches a fish there in no time. The mangrove forest used to be packed with crabs. You could walk past one billabong after another, all covered with lily pads. No land was kinder to its people and more plentiful with food than hers. Not any longer though.

The whites have built a settlement on the shore of the bay to melt the rocks. The place rattles, always puffing something, steam or smoke. Perhaps both. The stuff smells like a clutch of turtle's eggs turned bad and burst. You could be many camps out of sight but not out of reach of the stink. The water in the bay has grown yellow or reddish. I could not be sure, for there is always a haze hanging over it. There are no fish to be seen; they have long since been washed up on the shore, dead. The mangroves do not like the place either; the trees have shed their leaves, nothing but dry skeletons. I doubt whether they make darkguls and billy cans out at that smelter. There are not many of us left to need them anyway.

Not even Galei keeps a billy can. She had made her home in a discarded water tank on a rubbish heap not far from the white settlement. Her children looked much like her while they were still toddlers, but their skin looks lighter. Some even have freckles on their faces.

I see her often on my way to the jail, whenever I go there to fetch one of our fellows. At first I thought that one of our men might be wounded and need a good cure. That's what I am for. I always carry in my dilly bag some white bush lily to stop the bleeding and treat the wounds. It always turns out that it is too late for healing—the poor fellow is stiff dead. I think they call me there only to take the bodies of our fellows back into the bush. The whites do not want any of our kind to be buried on the land taken from us. Perhaps they fear that our people, when reborn, could claim the land again. Galei thinks so. She told me that if any of our fellows is found hanging around the white settlement he is thrown behind the lock. They would not lock her up though. The whites come to the rubbish heap to seek her company. Poor Galei—there is a whole mob of children flocking around her and there is always a new one on the way, by the look of her belly. She often came to see me in the bush, asking for iharang berry. I tried to tell her that Nongaru and much of the country around have been dug up. The sacred billabong has gone, so has the grove of the iharang bushes. The whites have turned the place into a mining quarry. It looks as though some monster, never seen before, has intruded on the place, crushed the boulders, and wallowed in the dust. It is still wallowing.

At sunset a blast is often heard from Nongaru. The earth jerks upward with a cloud of dust or smoke, one can never tell. Shaken, poor Wanga, our poor country, trembles like a badly wounded serpent. The dust cloud spits scattering rocks. They too travel across the land almost as far as the noise of the blast. I once saw a piece of wood flying into the air from Nongaru. Bent, it looked much like one of our sacred boomerangs smeared with blood. It fell halfway down the Nandjaranga Cape. Galei kept pleading: "You're the healer, do something to help."

I found an iharang bush among the rocks at the far end of the country. It looked stunned, the leaves coated with dust. The tree had no berries on it and looked unlikely ever to flower again. I took some bark from the bush and I pounded it with a rock before placing it in a bailer shell half-filled with water, and left the thing to soak. While he was around, Mari told me that if a woman drank stuff like that it would make her sick; she would recover after a while and go on to live, but without ever having children again. Poor Galei—she did not make it though.

That tribal ancestor Nagang no longer comes to ferry the souls of the dead to Bralgu. The rocks down at Nandjaranga Cape were blasted long ago. The noise from the blasts has frightened even the sea monster. The dreadful rotting smell from the smelter hangs in the air—our spirits would stay a sky away from Wanga. Galei is out in the bush, turned into a dingo. Last night she came close to me, looking for food in my camp. She sniffed the ground around me for the crumbs left behind from my last meal; for a while I felt her hairy tail touching my face. Before going to sleep next time, I shall leave her some yams and part of the bush bread cooked in hot ashes. She was fond of that tucker.

About fifteen or so years ago, the mining town of Gove was given the yuln name Nhulunbuy. The town has a large hospital, school, hotel—for whites. It also has a court-house, a police station, and a jail made of concrete in which aborigines are often locked.

A cape near Gove bears the name of William Wilberforce, the man who pioneered the Abolition of Slavery Act of 1833. The act supposedly gave rights to indigenous people over their land and culture. Lawyers in Australia are barred from referring to that legislation.

Nabalco nowadays pays some symbolic royalties to our people. We also receive government payments, pension or unemployment benefits. This money is often spent at Nhulunbuy paying police fines, or spent on alcohol, fast food, and other goods alien to our traditional life-style.

The world outside is no longer interested in our culture. People nowadays fly to Gove to compile reports on problems concerning aboriginal health, high mortality rates, alcoholism, death in police custody, and reports on pollution and environmental decay.

If the mining corporation ever leaves Gove, the bush might reclaim some of the devastated land. The same might not be true of our culture.

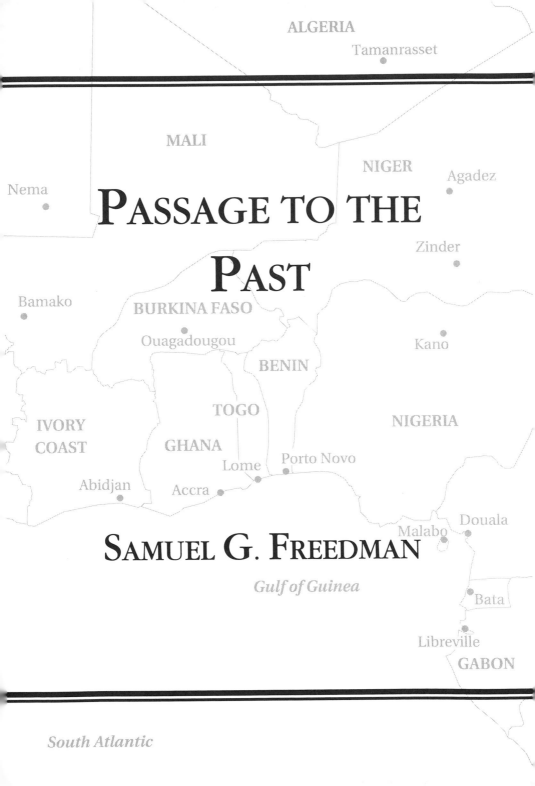

Passage to the Past

Samuel G. Freedman

Samuel G. Freedman was born in New York City and grew up in New Jersey. He holds a B.A. in history and journalism from the University of Wisconsin.

Mr. Freedman is the author of *Small Victories: The Real World of a Teacher, Her Students, and Their High School*, which was selected as a nonfiction finalist in the 1990 National Book Awards. He wrote the introductions to the books *Cousins and the Death of Papa*, and *A Chorus Line*. In addition, his work has been published in *Rolling Stone*, the *New York Times Magazine*, *New York Newsday*, the *Los Angeles Times*, and *Downbeat*. From 1981 to 1987 he was a reporter for the *New York Times*.

Mr. Freedman is currently McGraw Distinguished Professor of Writing at Princeton University. He lives in Metuchen, New Jersey, with his wife, Cynthia, and their son, Aaron.

The following selection is an excerpt from his forthcoming book *Upon This Rock: The Miracles of a Black Church*, to be published in February 1993 by HarperCollins.

Slowly the plane descends, riding the warm wind called the harmattan. Somewhere below, the savanna unfolds, the brown rivers run, the stone forts bear witness to commerce in slaves. Below wait Accra, and Ghana, and Africa. The Reverend Johnny Ray Youngblood, peering through his window, sees only night, night and the reflection of a boy across the aisle, wearily knotting his tie.

Turning his gaze back into the cabin, he sees the Ghanaians beginning to stir. Most sleep beneath wool overcoats, the clothing of diaspora in Brixton or the Bronx. Now they are returning home, to *kente* and palm wine, to families and villages they support from abroad. That indistinct land outside a dark window, the pastor knows, is supposed to feel like home to him, too.

He has come here, after all, for Saint Paul to seal a compact with its past in the form of a mission in the village of Asafo. But there are connections he represents beyond those of brick and mortar. On his way to the airport yesterday, the second of December, Dr. Youngblood found a woman waiting outside his study door. She pressed an envelope into his hands, and when he opened it hours later between planes in Amsterdam, he discovered a plea: "If you, Pastor, possibly could pay homage for so many of us, to the memories of our lost ancestors. Surely their souls cry out for our presence."

The words made him feel both proud and unworthy. It is Osei Yaw Akoto, his partner on this trip, who has made the pilgrimage before, who has traced his lineage back to a ship's log. The pastor was reared with the Africa of Tarzan. The nuns of his grammar school would scold a naughty black child, "You wild little African." Even the blues song counseled, "If you're white, you're alright. If you're brown, stick around. If you're black, get back. Get way back." And nothing in Dr. Youngblood's adulthood—not

Roots, not Malcolm X, not *Before the Mayflower*—could repair all the damage. He thinks now of Countee Cullen's question: "What's Africa to me?" Then he reaches into his shoulder bag, retrieves a sheet of shirt cardboard and a pen, and begins to write with the title, "The Middle Passage 371 Years Later."

Not by ship of wood,
But by ship of metal.
Not by water,
But by air.

Is this The Return?
So desired and so despaired about
By those who took the original trip?

O, Lord, have You now decided
That You will remember and respond
To the prayer of our fathers?
That You will remember Your covenant with them?

Am I a participant?
If so
Open mine eyes that I might see glimpses
of the truth Thou hast for me.

At noon on his first day in Africa, real Africa, Dr. Youngblood sits to lunch in a Chinese restaurant. Christmas tinsel dangles in loops from the ceiling, and a pop group, the Carpenters, sing carols on tape. The pastor shares the table with Osei and two Ghanaian friends, a genial pharmacist named Victor Aphreh, and Kwame Charles, a son of Asafo now parking cars in New York. It is Kwame, home for his first visit in five years, who has arranged a meeting after lunch with the village chief, a lawyer during the week with an office in Accra.

"Sometimes I'm embarrassed," Dr. Youngblood says to Victor and Kwame. "Because you African brothers think of us as being here." He raises a hand above his head. "And we're not." He drops his palm back to the table. "What do I have to say to African people? This is my first time. If this is home for me, I have to admit some of home is strange."

He had awakened at daybreak on the outer edge of the city, in the brick and mahogany home of a friend of Victor Aphreh's. Cinderblock houses covered the low land, and the once-green hills to the west had been shaved down to stubble. Still, the pastor thought he could feel Africa there—in the harmattan blowing, in thonged feet padding down roads, in the rhythmic thump of yam and plantain being pounded into *fufu,* the sound that Osei called "the heartbeat of Ghana."

More than anything, it was the soil that seemed to link Africa with his own life. He saw himself as a child, during Mississippi summers, playing in a yard of that selfsame red clay. He saw his Grandma Inola eating the rich dirt for health, and mixing it with water to apply to burns as a balm. He saw her walking from the fields, a basin of cucumbers balanced on her head, just like these women this morning carrying laundry or palm fronds.

But once Victor arrived and drove him deeper into Accra, the pastor's sense-memory grew quickly confused. He passed the Bronx Hair Salon and the theater called the Apollo, running the Arnold Schwarzenegger hit "Total Recall." Standing in line to change money, he heard the radio play "We're All in This Together," a song by David Peaston, a member of Saint Paul. And when he submitted his visa form to the immigration office, as all visitors must, the inspector corrected his answer on the "nationality" line. He left intact the word "American, " then drew his pen through its predecessor, its companion, "African."

Duality, though, was the inescapable truth. "One ever feels his two-ness," Dr. Youngblood had read in W. E. B. DuBois. "An American, a Negro; two souls, two thoughts, two unreconciled strivings; two warring ideals in one dark body." DuBois himself had journeyed to Ghana, to celebrate its independence and ultimately to die. He had finally found the identity toward which the pastor still gropes, with his sermons on how a village raises its children, with the ancestor chairs at Larry Johnson's wedding, with the bust of black Jesus in "the listening post." Perhaps Asafo would be where Africa met him halfway.

The chief, Barima Asante Abedi III, practices law above the bridal shop downtown. He wears wire-rim glasses and a blue suit that hangs limply in the heat. He has just returned from court, and the office is harried. Four piles of legal papers mount beneath metal weights. A secretary clatters out a brief on a manual typewriter. Two graying men in tribal robes arrive to discuss a land dispute, as bicycle bells and diesel fumes rise from the street.

Waiting his turn with Osei, Kwame, and Victor, Dr. Youngblood has already reached one decision. Saint Paul will not build a church in Asafo, for religion seems one resource in which Ghana abounds. Not a jitney rumbles through Accra without "The Name of God" on the windshield or "Deliver Me" above the bumper. There are businesses entitled Christ the King Motors and Psalm 106 Pipe Fittings. A single crossroads bears signs for churches led by Baptists, Presbyterians, Seventh Day Adventists, and Assemblies of God, so many the pastor joked to Osei, "It's like we never left Brooklyn." No, whatever Asafo needs from Saint Paul might have more to do with the children darting through traffic peddling sticks of gum, or the women lighting cooking fires next door to hotels, or the open sewers and open sores. The missionaries' message, Christianity as cure-all, was a failure and a lie.

Chief Abedi now welcomes the visitors into his office, thanks the pastor for previous donations of money and clothes. Dr. Youngblood, reciprocating, says, "I have come as a student. I have come looking. I am honored and I am humbled to come." He asks question after question, about customs of greeting and burial, about the easy way men walk holding hands, about the political legacy of Kwame Nkrumah, Ghana's founding father.

The chief belongs to the generation that was to rebuild modern Ghana, but has seen progress move with maddening leisure. Educated in law and economics in England, he presides over a village that only last year received electricity and still lacks enough medicine for its clinic or a high school within a fifteen-mile radius. "We are still ninety percent illiterate," he tells Dr. Youngblood.

"In Asafo?" the pastor asks.

"The whole country," Chief Abedi cries, throwing his hand toward the ceiling. "The whole country."

"Well, what if we could change that?" Dr. Youngblood says. "Even in one village?"

The chief nods, intrigued.

"I know there's been talk about a church," the pastor continues. "But one thing I do not want to do is build a church." He waits for objection; none comes. "Isn't it more important to have a school you've never had than one more church full of folk who can't read?"

"The concern of all Africa," Chief Abedi replies, "is to be better educated."

"Then this is the beginning."

But first, the chief insists, the pastor must visit Asafo. This Sunday the village will hold a *durbar*, a festival, in his honor. There will be dancing and eating and singing and ceremony. And when the revelry ends, there will be daylight enough to find a site for a school.

I look for some click,
Some reminder, some moment of déjà vu.
Some all-focusing, resurrecting, cataclysmic birth
That answers all questions, fills all the gaps.
I hope, I wish, I hallucinate.

Once Victor Aphreh's car pushes free of Accra, bound east on the Cape Coast Highway, the face of Africa softens from corrugated tin to palm thatch. Fishing villages perch on the oceanside bluffs, and in the surf shirtless men hoist nets heavy with the day's catch. Yet here, where the foreign hand seems most absent, white men first came to shore. They called this land "The Mine" for its abundance of gold, a commodity soon supplanted by prisoners of war. And indeed, as the car turns into the town of Elmina, the columns and louvers of Europe appear. Past the church with its bell tower and across the softly arched bridge stands the reason for this settlement, the Castle of Saint George.

Its double moat dry, its cannons long silent, the castle now serves only as a museum. But for more than four centuries its purpose was profit. In its most efficient years, Saint George alone warehoused and shipped ten thousand slaves, nearly fifteen percent of the continent's annual total. So lucrative was business that the Dutch, having captured the castle from its Portuguese founders, erected a second fortress to protect their investment. Britons, Swedes, Germans, French, Danes—all competed in the trade, building castles of their own along a 150-mile coast.

"Every time I come here, I get something deeper," says Osei, who has visited twice before, as he steps from the car. "Something that fills a void that's been in me for a long time."

"I can't figure how I'm supposed to feel," Dr. Youngblood says. "I'm more than a tourist. This is history. Our history. But how do you get angry at something so huge?"

"Wait till you get inside," Osei says as they walk toward the gate. "Inside is rough."

They enter a stone plaza surrounded by thick white-washed walls. It resembles, fittingly enough, a medieval village square, for the fortress once housed its own masons and tailors, coopers and blacksmiths. Even a priest practiced here, in the castle's private church, above whose door was inscribed a verse from Psalm 132: "For the Lord hath chosen Zion to be a habitation for himself: It is his dwelling place forever."

Only a series of unlit tunnels lead to the cells where the captives were held. Hearing voices, Dr. Youngblood and the rest follow down one, joining the castle's sole tour guide, who is already leading a few Europeans. Just now, he is pointing into a windowless room, adorned by the portrait of a man wearing *kente* and an unrepentant glare. He is Prempeh I, the Ashanti king who mounted a rebellion against Ghana's British rulers in the late 1800s. Slavery being illegal by then, the British punished him with prison, followed by exile, only to see the Ashanti queen take the insurrection's reins.

Around a corner and through an archway, the guide comes to a square room, perhaps twelve feet by thirty, the dungeon that held up to two hundred women. They received food through an iron gate and air from a single two-foot-square hole. They had neither toilets nor pallets for sleep. The routine varied for only the most mutinous women, who were beaten in a courtyard and then chained to cannon balls. From a terrace above, officers chose their sexual victims.

"Remember that boy yesterday?" Osei asks Dr. Youngblood.

He refers to a child they had passed in Accra, whose tawny skin and loose curls had puzzled the pastor, here in a pure-blooded black nation.

51

"Now you know why," Osei says with dry disgust.

Behind the guide, they now squeeze through a tunnel and into the chamber that held men. It is a damp and nearly lightless room with the upward curved ceiling that suggests a wine cellar. But the place carries a harsh and bittersweet smell, as if the scent of black bodies had worked its way forever into the mortar and stone.

"This is the sole exit," the guide says. He indicates a window as tall as his waist, wide as his arm from elbow to wrist. Through it can be seen a cove and the pilings left from a pier. The captives, it is clear, could see the ships that would take them away. "The Portuguese built it small so no one could escape," the guide continues. "When the boats were ready, they were pushed through, one at a time."

Dr. Youngblood asks a question about resistance or rebellion. And the guide, by way of answer, leads the group across the plaza. He halts outside a single cell, ten feet high and wide and deep, marked above its entrance with the crossbones and skull. "This was for the leaders," he explains. "They would starve them to death."

Only several strides from the cell stands a church, built for worship by the Portuguese but used as a slave market by the British and Dutch. Here victorious tribes sold their prisoners into bondage on an altar transformed into an auction block; here money was counted in what had been confessionals. "It's enough," Dr. Youngblood says to Osei, "to turn you against religion."

They climb from the plaza to an apartment inside the west bastion of the castle. By the standards used for Africans, these rooms could have housed hundreds; but only a handful lived here, the governor and his family. They had beds and chairs and wide windows overlooking the surf, the trappings that even today evoke a resort.

Afterwards, atop the battlement, nobody speaks. Dr. Youngblood leans forward, regarding the ocean and the palm-shaded beach, the last piece of Africa the captives ever saw. The sound of chirping laughter suddenly rises from below. In a rocky tidal pool, three village boys are playing, splashing each other with seawater until their naked bodies gleam. Dr. Youngblood spots them and waves.

For all its mass scale, genocide was a deeply personal crime—one kidnapping, one murder, committed millions of times. The sight of those boys reminds the pastor of a family story. Generations back on his mother's side, seven brothers had mistakenly cut wood on a white man's property. Over days they were hunted down, left to die in the fields, only one escaping barefoot down the road to New Orleans. And from the time Ottie Mae told him, at the age of thirteen, Johnny never asked her another question about Reconstruction or slavery. Until today, in a sense, disbelief and helplessness and fear had conquered memory.

Without words, Dr. Youngblood and the others walk to the museum's office. There, covered with sweat and salt spray, they sign the visitors' register. In the column headed "Impressions," a Dane has written, "Have a good day," followed by a Swiss with the comment, "I would not mind having a bedroom view like the governor."

Dr. Youngblood reads their words, struck but not surprised at the lack of compassion. He remembers the aftermath of the racial murders in Howard Beach and Bensonhurst, when whites questioned about bigotry told reporters, "My family never owned slaves." So he writes of his day at the Castle of Saint George, "Though horrible and hateful, it keeps the history alive." And he says to Osei, as they return to the car, "To survive all this, it must have been for *something*."

If you're my real folk, resonate for me.
Home seems strange when you've been away,
Family seems different when you've been apart.

Is there no place like home?
Is home where the heart is?
Do I have a heart?
Or was it lost in the Middle Passage?

Five miles off the main road from Accra to Kumasi, surrounded by palms and banana groves, the village of Asafo sits hunched on a hilltop. It appears, amid the greenery, as a palette of earth tones—the red-brown of rusting tin roofs, the burnt orange of ferric soil, the pale mustard of mud walls, the beige of bamboo fences, protecting every precious cashew tree.

The town seems nearly deserted as Dr. Youngblood and Osei Yaw arrive late on a Saturday afternoon. Three boys shoot marbles. Two barefoot girls sell mirrors and locks from a wood stand. A bush taxi bounces through town, past the Otargo Trading Agency and the Looking Cute Beauty Base, kicking up clouds of red dust.

"Akwaba," says a graying man in green *kente*, the village captain, greeting the visitors in the language of Twi.

"Medasi," says Dr. Youngblood, thank you. He has been practicing for this moment all week.

Most of the people, the captain explains, are attending a funeral on the outskirts of town. Dr. Youngblood and Osei will be taken to the ceremony, formally introduced to the chief and his court. But first, there are rituals to be observed, of welcome and return.

The captain, whose name is Edward Bismarck Adjebemj, leads Osei and the pastor through a gap between two stores, down a gully, across a creek, and onto the back porch of his home. Kwame Charles joins them, bare-chested, wrapped in cloth from waist to shin, only his camera carried over from New York. He will serve as Dr. Youngblood's "linguist," the interlocutor who in Ghanaian culture represents any man of position. Two boys enter the yard lugging an iron pot of palm wine and a calabash cup. As the captain speaks in Twi, the other men adding words of assent, he ladles wine from pot to calabash, spills several drops on the ground. He is "pouring libation," in the Ghanaian phrase, beseeching the ancestors to intercede with the divine.

"Kwame," Dr. Youngblood whispers, "tell me some of what he said."

"He prays to God and Mother Earth for your safe arrival," Kwame explains. "It is good you have come to Asafo to see things for yourself. God should help you. And if bad spirits try to stop you, then the ancestors should punish them. The ancestors should always protect you."

A boy brings the calabash to Osei. He spills a drop, touches the wine to his sober lips without swallowing, spills a bit more. Then Dr. Youngblood, to applause, drains the vessel. The wine tastes like sour orange juice, and it is covered with foam that must be wiped free of flies. None of that matters now. "Come," the captain says, pointing the way toward the funeral. "Let us rise."

At the dirt crossroads that marks the center of town, the men turn west into the setting sun. As they pass the rural bank and the lottery kiosk and the children peddling ground nuts and brown eggs, the raucous pulse of high-life music reaches toward them, summoning. Its source is the funeral, an affair not of sorrow but celebration, and an occasion when ancient and modern easily mesh.

The man who died, Okyeane Kwaku Ottum, was at eighty-five the most senior and esteemed of Chief Abedi's four linguists. Hundreds of villagers have gathered in tribute, the dignitaries on a raised concrete platform, the families beneath a palm thatch pavilion. High-life pours from two speakers and a tape deck, all cooled by a whirling fan. Across the clearing sit four drummers, awaiting their time, each with a crooked staff at the ready. Some villagers dance in the open space, while others carry money to the collectors seated on the podium. Half will be given to the linguist's survivors and half held for the donor's clan association in two parallel expressions of mutual aid.

"I got thirty million questions in my head," Dr. Youngblood says to Kwame, but the funeral is beginning to surrender to twilight. Its joyous spirit reminds the pastor of the phrase he employs at Saint Paul, not "funeral" but "homegoing celebration." The syncopated procession, as it heads back into town, resembles nothing so much as the New Orleans jazz funerals of his childhood, with their "second-line" meter and swaying umbrellas, just like the one the chief carries now. It was one thing to study and speak about "African retentions," another to see one march before your eyes.

Asafo, it is clear, works as Accra never will. Whatever its material wants, it is an African place with a time-honored logic, not a European imposition struggling to adapt. Even Chief Abedi, who looked so beleaguered and put-upon in his law office, exudes a kind of radiance here. Gone are the glasses, the suit, the yellowing papers. He wears ebony *kente* with a red sash across one shoulder and a string of cowrie shells. His body looks supple, muscular, young.

Although the *durbar* will not be held until tomorrow, Dr. Youngblood will be officially announced now. Kwame leads him into the courtyard of the chief's palace, a weathered brick building two stories tall. The pastor shakes hands with the courtiers, then, through his linguist, addresses the chief.

"Osei Yaw, my brother, came to Ghana and Asafo last year in search for his roots," he says. "And he returned to us with the message that there were needs we could meet as African-Americans and Christians. So this trip is for me, so I can go home and tell my people what we can do."

There is applause as Kwame translates.

"In the five days I have been in Ghana, I have seen

enough churches. At this point, I am not interested in a church, but more so a school. It is our desire to build a secondary school in Asafo."

Kwame translates again, adding at the end the Twi words for, "Education first."

When the clapping subsides, Chief Abedi speaks.

"The people of Asafo thank you for your speech and your happiness," he says. "When we look at your face, we know you are not from America. You are from here."

Later in the evening, they talk more, and more privately. They sit on folding chairs on the porch of the chief's house, lit by kerosene lamps. From his godfather in New Orleans to William Jones in Brooklyn, all of Johnny Ray Youngblood's elders were familiar with his unquenchable curiosity. Now, amid all the sounds of crickets and rustling leaves, Chief Abedi fields the first of innumerable questions, all of which add up to one question, "What is my reason for being?"

"I remember about twenty-five years ago," the chief says, "Louis Armstrong came here. And when he played trumpet, a woman started dancing, and Louis Armstrong said she looked like his mother. He hugged her. So when we see American blacks, we see our brothers and sisters. You look like us. It is a chain."

But the chain, if not broken, was strained and warped by abduction. And as a Christian, a black Christian familiar with the unsparing analysis of Malcolm X, the pastor wonders aloud if he is practicing "the religion of the oppressor." The other day in Accra, in fact, he had laughed bitterly at a cartoon painted on a truck's tailgate. Two mice were regarding a trap baited without cheese. "And they call themselves Christians," one muttered.

"When the white missionaries first came," Chief Abedi replies, "they gave us the idea that our beliefs were no good, paganism. They made us discard them. They made us swallow their religion." He clears his throat. "But now we vomit. We have African theologians, and we are fashioning a Christianity to suit our conditions. We remember and honor the dead ancestors. For what they have achieved and what they have set aside for us. We want to keep our bond."

"Have you ever forgiven the white man?" Dr. Youngblood asks, thinking not only of enforced Christianity but of the Castle of Saint George.

"Slavery was heinous, but we also think in retrospect we, too, are partly to blame. We should not have sold our own people, captured our own brothers, for cloth or rum. We, too, are morally culpable."

The talk turns to the proposed school. And the more Chief Abedi speaks of the need for practical training, particularly in agriculture and public health, the more Dr. Youngblood thinks of Booker T. Washington's Tuskegee. Finally, they reach the subject of money. To build a facility for six hundred children, the chief says, would cost $15,000. Dr. Youngblood, shocked, tells him that in New York $15,000 might purchase one child one year of college.

"If I know my people," he says, "unless things have changed a lot since I left, you've got your $15,000."

In the amber lamplight, Chief Abedi's hands move, palm striking palm in soft, sincere thanks.

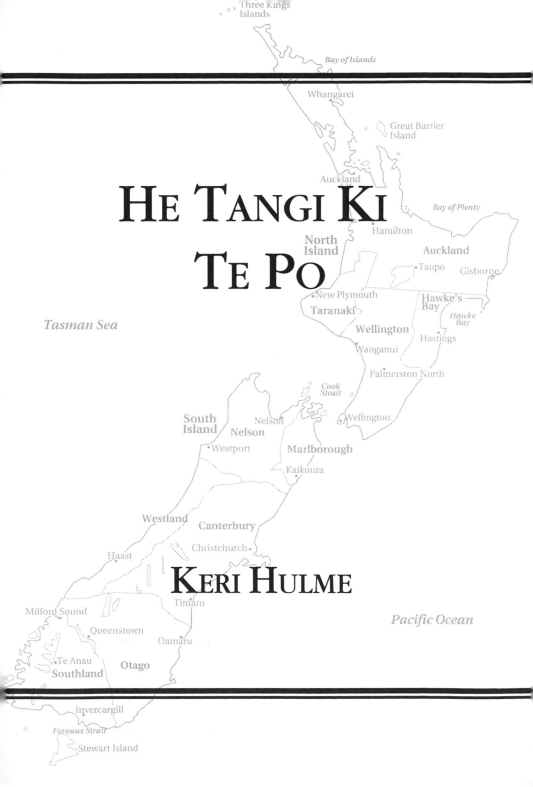

HE TANGI KI
TE PO

Tasman Sea

KERI HULME

Pacific Ocean

Keri Hulme was raised in Christchurch and Moeraki, New Zealand. She is a Maori writer and painter.

Ms. Hulme is the author of *The Bone People*, for which she was awarded the Booker Prize in 1985; *Te Kaihau: The Windeater*; a book of short stories; and three collections of poetry.

The following selection, "He Tangi Ki Te Po" (Crying in the Night), is an excerpt from her forthcoming novel *Bait*, which will be published in the United States by Viking Penguin.

Ms. Hulme lives in Okarito, Westland, New Zealand.

*T*he following selection is a fictional account of an elderly woman, Moitoitoi Miller, the last surviving member of the Kati Tio people. In mourning the death of the boy to whom she had hoped to pass on the heritage of the Kati Tio, she recalls her own childhood.

THE FIRST THINGS I CAN REMEMBER
are lying in silky-soft grass, and the smell of smoke.

The grass was my bedding for my first two years, muka really, not grass. Taua had teased it from the flax leaves, and pounded it, washed it many times...it was like lying on golden hair, only without the scratchy tickle of hair. And I liked lying on *it*. I had a blanket of course, but often it was over me, not round me...just me and my fine grass bed together, keeping each other warm.

It is always a shock to touch the hands of the dead.

The scent of smoke was everywhere. Even Taua and Poua smelt of smoke, not because they were dirty but because the smoke permeated everything, even us. It didn't hang round, there weren't drifts of it inside the whare, though it would swirl about a bit above the hearth if someone slid the door. And it wasn't cooking smoke, oh no. Taua was very traditional—cooking fire in the kauta, fire in the home only for warmth and cheerfulness. When I think about that kauta, I want to cry. She didn't have a range, my taua, she didn't have frypans or kettles or pots, just an old iron goashore that Poua's father had got off a whalerman...you see, it was all steamed, boy, steamed or boiled our food. Soups and fish-stews and birds in the goashore, oh they were so lovely, sweet meat. And potatoes and turnips too, Poua grew them in the summer garden. I mind the way we used all the turnip, washed and ate the roots, ate the tops...pora, they were called, pora. Like the people who brought them here, takata-pora, the ship people...it was so funny, tamait', when I went to school and learned what the takata-pora thought of themselves! "The Maori gazed in awe at this wondrous craft. Surely it is a vessel of the Gods, they said." Well no, actually, we could see the crew were humans, a bit odd looking but definitely human. And they brought some useful things, like little round white vegetables. Takata-pora...ah boy, there is so much *more* to tell you.

> Charlie said you were
> cuddled into the sand, as
> though you were cold and
> wanted it a blanket over you.

My grandfather wasn't bothered by takata-pora, he didn't have any fear of them. What did worry him was people from the North.

"They have always come in angry waves," he said, "and like sand dunes before a stormy sea, we have always given way."

He is sitting cross-legged before the fire, and I am leaning against his heart-side shoulder. He is wearing just his maro, so his shoulder is smooth and warm under my arm. For so old a man, his skin is a surprise: he is wrinkled heavily at his knees and elbows, and face, but his body is still firm. I smell the smoke, and love his dark brown eyes. Am I six? Seven? Somewhere round that age.

"We were here in the beginning, when the birds were huge and we were the only people. It was very mild then, we didn't have frosts and we could grow kumura beyond Otepoti. There was plenty of good soft food, but it all changed. The weather grew harsh, and other people began arriving from the North."

I shiver. I know this story. This is why there is only me

and my grandparents left in all the world. This is why we are all there is of Kati Tio.

"There were only a few of them at first, and we felt sorry for them. We showed them how rich this island was, how succulent and easy to catch the fish, how fat and sweet the birds. We showed them how we made our gardens still produce, even in the colder weather. We told them which rocks were alive, where the good—and bad—taniwha were. We took them into our families." He sighs. "But there were more and more of them, and they considered themselves apart, even when married amongst us. So we withdrew, a little. The land is large. There was room for us all. It seemed however that they could not be easy except they had *all* the land. They thrived, they grew great, and they harried us. And we—maybe because in sharing our secrets with them, we had given away too much—we were diminishing. There were fewer families each generation in the round of kai-haukai. This did not move Gati Laki to pity. They pursued us, enslaved us when they could. Even when the next wave of Gati Laki came, the ones who call themselves the Fire People, they did not stop harassing us. And Ngati Ahi joined with them—when they weren't fighting among themselves."

There are veins like tiny eels on his temples: they creep back under his silver hair. He puts his arm around me, and holds me closer, so my shivering will stop.

"We weren't great ones for fighting. We were too precious to each other, too few together, to ever have practiced war. If we argued—well, we'd just go our separate ways until the argument didn't seem important any more. The season-al feasts helped. It was hard to keep a quarrel alive when you were fat and happy. But the Gati Laki used the kai-haukai like they were another kind of war. You provided ten poha of birds? We will have twenty ready for you, and the best quality of bracken root besides...beat that! We couldn't of course, there weren't enough of us to do the work. In anyway we didn't want to ruin our feasts. So we retreated to the margins of the land. Here, my Motoitoi, where there are sharks in the cavern in spring and we can cull the weka runs in autumn. Katigi on the coast, our winter home, where I harvest the penguin chicks and the titi, and your grandmother gathers kareko and rimurapa. You remember Katigi from last year?"

Do I answer Yes? I remember the kareko and the rimurapa, especially the latter because Taua made me a treat from it, trimming off the holdfasts and roasting the thick little stems on embers until they blackened. How many days did she leave them in running water? I can see her taking the basketful out of the stream and stripping off the black and swollen outer skin: I can taste the chewy sweet chunks of takapau, seaweed liquorice, boy...it was takapau?

"and on Tai Poutini, the Eye of the Taniwha is our last hold," says Poua faintly, "remember it for safety, Eye of the Taniwha."
     I am losing him from my mind's eye again. His voice has faded, the sea is too loud, the glint of his eyes in firelight is a distant star now, the pale gleam of his maro turned to the sand I crouch on.

I huddle into the sand, e aki, I huddle. I wanted you to know this place like I know it, not just with my senses, not just through my skin. I wanted you to have the names and the stories, as well as all the provender, the abundance of my lagoon. I wanted so much for you to

share our spirit here, so Kati
Tio would not be finally
dead when I go into the
night.
    Instead you're lying at Francis' house, your clever blunt
fingers slack—

Take out Taua's jade knife: it is smoother than skin to touch,
but as lively. It has been handled, used, for—I don't know
how many years, I only know how many people. Me,
Mahola, Matakiore, Te Rare, right back to Te Tieke, the
woman who fought the great eagle, the woman for whom
you were made, o Kuraparihi. You are not a large thing,
your back long and thick as my forefinger, your back with
the twelve grooves in it. There is the fracture flake, which
has never lifted all these years, and the waisted hole at the
other end that Te Amaru bored for his senior wife Tu-
wharemea so she could wear the knife round her neck. As
we all have worn it round our necks since. You are an
ancient and beautiful halfmoon, Kuraparihi, and your pale
curving edge has been loved by thirteen of us over the
centuries. Thirteen of us, all told, who have done the
practical things with your help, skinning and carving birds
and fish, and who have done the ritual things. This, this, and
this—

The blood comes slowly at first, as though my heart isn't
working properly, but the next cuts must hit little veins for
look it spurts, runnelling under that breast, sluicing down
that arm…they flange back like tiny mouths sucking at the
night…my eyes should be bleeding, that is where the aches
are, there and in my throat—
    I will light the fire soon.
    There are so many dead.

*   *   *

Did we do something wrong in not fighting back? We tried once, in the garden known as Bright Mist, when Gati Laki came to raid the harvest. Our men fought with hoe and digger, our women fought with bracken-root pounders and stones. Taua said the very children fought. And all the result was that whole family of Kati Tio was killed or enslaved. They were lost in the Northerners, leaving so few of us…boy, I know I go on and on about how it was, how we were, I cannot say hello without explaining how we used to say it. But I won't believe an entire people became shadows, with nobody to remember truly who we were…I tried passing it all on to Amokura, but he. Never. Never heard what I said, it seemed. It is getting hard to breathe. Maybe it was because he was half foreign, more foreign than the takata-pora. Maybe. Was I wrong to delay mourning for him? But I was not certain, I am still not certain, what he wanted…and if I showed grief, other people would realize he was dead. And ask how I knew he was dead. And ask where he was.

Francis says it is illegal what he wanted, may have wanted, what we've done. I only know it is wrong. But it is too late to worry about that now.

The night is cold about me, wrapping this bare old torso in numbness. Tau! Thank you, night! The sand is chill under my feet. They're not numb. I've walked the world barefoot too long for them to ever be less than responsive to her. And I've searched this tahuna with my toes so often, it must be like home for them. You know it is named, e aki? It was a proverb, the never-fail food-house…but then we named everything. That stone, this tree, that hillock, this creek…aue, so much to tell you. You could bring me to a rage by not hearing things, but these last few months, you *were* listening, the words were going in.

> The water has done
> something strange to your
> face, as though it has washed
> out the man you were

> becoming to show the child
> you were.
> Charlie said nothing had been
> at you. He said that when he
> lifted you, water ran out, that
> was all.

If I keep thinking old time, maybe now will go away. Poua said that could happen, that you could go forward along the line of ancestors and rest in them, and they in you. Well, my taua, you must be closest to me after Pou', come to my sandbank, crouch with me and keen...but that is the birds. Why is it oystercatchers with us? And white herons? The torea haunt our birth and dying, the kotuku let us know death is coming. One came by for you e kui, and one for Amokura's father, and yesterday, searching along the north beach, I rested my eyes from the waves in the green of that stand of trees that looms by Kohuamaru Bluff. Their tops were lost in mist, the day was all mist, but as I watched, the cloud round one treetop coiled and solidified, became the shining bird too white for the eyes to easily note its shape. The kotuku tangi'd, the harsh cry broke on me, and then the bird swept into the air, flew over my head towards the sea and turned hard left as I knew it would. That is the aitua, that is the sign. Its slow deliberate beautiful wing beat powered the bird on, chest-prow forward then lost in the mist. I knew he was dead then, Taua, I knew he had to be dead.

Do you remember the little girl who stroked your arms and asked what the white marks were? Touched the seams traversing your thin breasts? And you saying, "Grief cuts, as this is a grief earring," holding forward the long gray-green pendant. Your lobe is so stretched that I can put my little finger in the hole. I do. "Grief?" I ask. "Tears and pain for your mother, e 'Toi, for she who was my daughter. And for my parents before her, there and

67

there, and a sister I had, long ago," fingering the silvered scars across her upper arms. "She was killed by a disease the takata-pora brought with them, like your mother." I know all about the maremare: it's the other reason the 15 last Kati Tio became just my grandparents and me. I am more interested in this tracery of grief upon my taua. "Didn't they hurt, the cuts?" She sighs, and sits me down on her lap to cuddle me close. "Not enough, my 'Toi, not enough."

And child that I was, I thought that funny. Not until I grieved for her and Poua did I learn you can't cut the pain out, that wounds are only good for diffusing the unbearable ache of death.

A torea calls wheep wheep to my right. Sandhoppers are skittering round the dark drops on the sand. They think it food, it *is* food…the cuts have stopped dribbling now, they are going sticky, a strange varnish on my chest and arm. I stand and groan at the pain of standing and realize I have not tangi'd yet at all. The torea are calling for me, a flock of them nestled onto the sand five yards away. They do not shift when I limp into the water, and wash Kuraparihi, and hang him back cold round my neck. Nor do they move when I take the kindling out from my kit and build and light the little fire.

Across the lagoon, Francis' house is ablaze with all the lights on.
She will be sat beside you, holding your indifferent hand, house and woman fighting back the night.

Here, the pale flames echo the curve of my knife: the inhuman weeping from the oystercatchers resounds back of my eyes. In four more hours, dawn will come.

I burn the words I made, closing and proscribing Takiri

river and beach. I burn the greenery (the little fire hisses and spits) that signified to those who don't use words, Takiri waters are forbidden. It's all clean again, Takaroa, because you have given him back, we are open and free once more.

Open and free, hah! Open to ill-luck and free to die—not you, Takaroa, I am not saying this to you. I cannot loose the grief gnawing at my throat, I cannot howl into this liminal dark GIVE HIM BACK GIVE THEM BACK GIVE US ALL BACK TO ME—

if Francis were beside me, she would understand that wordless shriek, she would balance this end of my sandbank, even as Poua and Taua and the now-silent birds weigh down the other.

The little fire is dying.

The bitter ripples of the outgoing tide wash against my feet.

And the big woman standing there waist-deep in the lagoon, her child lofted against one broad shoulder, the big woman says,

"Toi, come home with me. We are living, and only the dead people this place."

> You are gone into the night,
> and it is too late, too late.

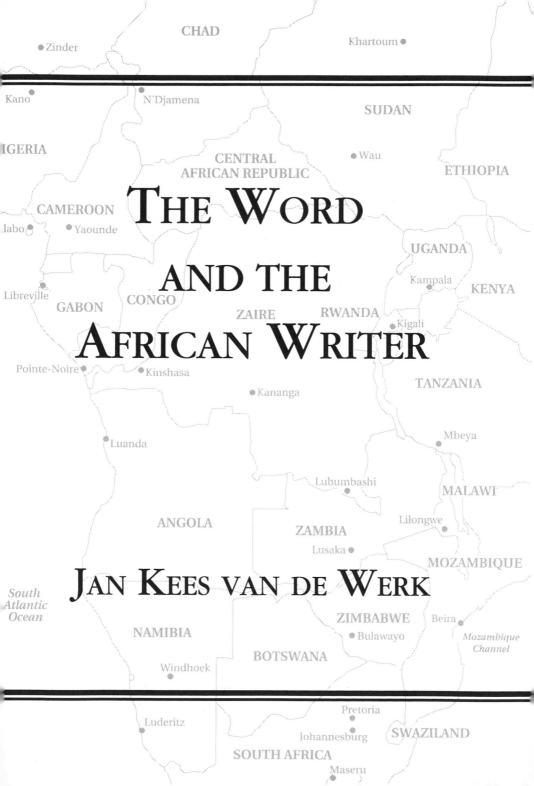

THE WORD

AND THE

AFRICAN WRITER

JAN KEES VAN DE WERK

J an Kees van de Werk was born in Utrecht, the Netherlands. He has lived and traveled throughout Africa, and was instrumental in setting up the African Publishers Network and other related publishing projects in Africa. In 1980 he launched *Afrikaanse Bibliotheek*, an ongoing series of African literature in Dutch translation.

Mr. van de Werk has written numerous articles on African literature which in 1992 won him the Scherpenzeel Prize, a journalism award for outstanding work illuminating North-South relations. He lives in 's Graveland, the Netherlands, with his wife, Els, and their two daughters, Leonoor and Sanne.

Chenjarai Hove was born in Zimbabwe in 1956. He has written works for the theater as well as several novels, including *Bones,* which won the Noma Award in 1989, and *Shadows.* Mr. Hove's work has been published in Zimbabwe and England.

Werewere Liking was born in Cameroon in 1950. Ms. Liking is a writer and choreographer. She has written three novels, two plays, and two collections of initiation stories. Her work has been published in Senegal and France.

The Western idea of African literature and Africa is still dominated by prejudices ranging from an illiterate stammering on paper to images of a dehydrated continent lost between AIDS and a military coup. This perspective overlooks the rich vein of oral history running through African societies and the wealth of performance tradition, much of which has been entrusted to paper only recently.

Part of the problem can be traced to the journalistic reporting about North-South relationships, highly determined as it is by the rules of news-gathering. As a result, non-Africans are often shown only a flat, monochrome slice of the rounded, multicolored reality. The tinkling of coins from the African literary treasure trove are drowned out by the monotonous—albeit well-intentioned—rattle of the collection-box.

I spoke with the African writers Chenjerai Hove and Werewere Liking about imagination and reality, the role of literature, and their relation to the word as medium as it is expressed in an oral culture, and the way in which they as writers do justice on paper to the spoken power of the word.

*   *   *

© Jan Kees van de Werk

The work of Chenjerai Hove consists of poetry, novels, and radio plays and expresses everyday, though no less dramatic, situations and feelings: drought, expectations, oblivion, dreams, and hope. His texts are permeated with the smells, the rhythm, and the landscape of Zimbabwe.

My mother was one of the best storytellers in the village. That was back before the radio killed her voice, a voice we identified with the night. She was the actor, the storyteller who sang and danced, and also allowed us to tell stories. Every night she was the center of the children's lives. They brought her firewood to warm her while she related every imaginable adventure from the lives of the people and the animals. She never told a story the same way twice. She breathed new life into a story with each telling.

This African storytelling tradition directly influences the modern writer, particularly where forms of style are concerned. There are ways of leading a story along oral pathways that are almost impossible to avoid; that is because we are a society more attuned to passing on stories by word of mouth than we are a reading community.

Today, oral literature plays a completely different role in Africa. Children no longer sit by the fire listening to their grandmother tell stories, depicting them with every trick of the theater. But there are rituals and traditional ceremonies in which the song is so fluid that the melody is the only thing you're certain of. The words change every day, according to the situation.

I think that words alone are poor instruments with which to express emotion. They do have the power to bear a little of feelings, thoughts, and aspirations. But they are usually inadequate. Consequently, there is a great difference between the written word and the word in a story told aloud. Writing is recording; speaking is performing, sweating out expression. The page confines the story within the limited meanings of the word as defined in the dictionary. The reminiscence, the oral story is fluid, flexible, and profuse in using words until they are threadbare and then trading them in for new, fresh words when the situation requires. In oral tradition the story remains intact, for the storytellers continually enrich the same old story with new words. The word is always kept company by the totality of the performance: by dance, song, by the participation of the audience and of the night in which the story is told.

Literature must be enjoyed, just like any other performance. Every text is like a piece of music, yearning for ears to hear it. My "ears" are the people who dare to read when it would be more interesting to talk. Maybe they have the money to buy a book, maybe not. Books are not exactly a priority in my country. Flour must be bought for the next meal, the children need shoes before school begins again. Nor do I pretend that our people should not first provide themselves with the necessities of life or that they should buy books while their bellies are rumbling from hunger and disease. I also accept the reality of the feeble urbanite who is overwhelmed by other, more powerful and pitiless cultural products that seduce him into distancing himself from his own culture.

For a writer, text is also a dialogue with oneself. The writer discovers the characters, and the characters discover the writer. The result of all writing is self-knowledge. There is no reason whatsoever to boast. Writing makes you humble— the humility of having experienced it, of having been a witness. Sometimes you are successful in relating a story, sometimes you fail.

As a writer, the written word frightens me. Writing is loaded with fear because our people cannot read, although they have mastered the art of the spoken word. They are artists of the word who hate the scantier character of the written word. I have written my novels in a language that is also a voice of my people. But I know that those who inspired me will not read them. That is why I also feel the pain of exile within myself, far removed from the oral tradition, far away from how we used language as we were growing up. The imagination is trapped in a twofold alienation; that of language, with which it struggles to express reality, and that of the polyphonic reality itself, which reveals itself only through all the intonations of oral expression.

Despite the fact that we are not a reading community, I believe that the philosophies of our people must be set down in the pages of literature. The legends of our people, which reconstruct our collective history, will compel us all to humility. We must understand that history, the true history, is primarily humility. Our stories are part of the ongoing history of our people, who gave us life.

History cannot be the skeleton of the leftovers of reality we read in the authorized history books. I am history myself, walking on two legs. I walk through remembrance, the history of our breath, on many invisible legs. We inherit struggle after struggle.

In an age of daily pain and suffering, art for the sake of art is a useless pastime. I want a hoe, a pen to weed the consciousness of my people, the consciousness of history. We live in a struggle for possession, for refusal, breath, rebellion, for harmony. Harmony with the rules of the inherited breath, rebellion against the decline, so that those who inherit our breath will say: "The past is the rebellious future we inherited for our children."

A man of letters can allow himself to be forgetful, for his memories are stored outside him, in libraries. Someone from an oral culture will not forget so quickly; life and survival stand or fall with remembering.

We are the children of remembrance. We are the remembering itself. We must not fall asleep. To sleep is to fall into decay, to give the novel—the bearer of our memories—the opportunity to fade away, to die like a child in our arms. How can we sleep when we know that history never rests for a moment? The globe is always awake, pushing on us, on this continent, to the edges of time. History rolls on with the power of the pangs of childbirth, irresistible and full of yearning for the birth of the baby. History surges in the breath, already present at the beginning of the remembrance I have inherited. I write as a witness to the remembrance and the experience.

The creation of the mouth coincided with the creation of the memory. When Adam said: "The woman Thou hath placed at my side, she has given me from the tree and I have eaten," he was already living it in remembrance. His time was not measured by ticking watches, but in experience, in remembering. The story, the novel, is also remembering.

For me, fiction does not exist. I want to write about the reality that people have the impertinence to call fiction. The "fiction" I write is history now. Unfortunately, the greater part of the history of the powerless has never been written down. Those who command power over the rifle, the pen, and the capital decide who our heroes are. Those who colonized Zimbabwe described us, ignoring our diversity, as beasts who were to be either converted or exterminated.

The name Zimbabwe is taken from the great stone monuments built centuries ago by our ancestors. The colonialists decided that these monuments could never be the work of the people they had just defeated. They wrote the history books, and in them they denigrated our people so that we could barely recognize ourselves. A people denied its history is a people deprived of its humanity...and its cultural expression, with which history is expressed.

© Jan Kees van de Werk

The writer and choreographer Werewere Liking writes novels, poetry, plays, and essays; she makes films, paints, and manipulates the strings of her marionettes throughout the world. Exploring the frontiers of a variety of literary genres, she effects crosscurrents between the various forms of prose and poetry.

I take issue with the clichéd approach to Africa as a lost continent without a past or future.

I have always said that colonization has brought about irreparable damage to Africa. The colonialists convinced us that we have no perception of the world and that we have never been in touch with the power of creation. How can people without their own perception of God be complete?

Then they were kind enough to offer us a Judeo-Christian image of God, an image that clashed somewhat with our vision of the world. But we had been defeated, so the other god was more powerful. We had to obey him, a white god in whose image we had been created. As taught to us, he was a megalomaniac god, morbid and irritable. A god who worked six days to create the world and has been resting ever since. A god who does not tolerate the slightest questioning, who punishes offenses to the fourth generation with fire, earthquake, and flood.

This despotic image of god—and the fact that it was imposed on us by peoples who enslaved us—goes a long way to explain the dictatorships, the nepotism, the unfairness and intolerance under which we suffer in Africa today, with nothing to offset them. The loss of our culture and the influence of the imposed cultures have been disastrous. Power in Africa is in the hands of the divine dictators and sectarianism. Our "infallible" leaders model the nations, to which they play father for the rest of their lives, and then they rest. Like the white god, they tolerate only praise and total submission. Every thought, every comment, every question is regarded as subversive. There is no room whatsoever for creativity or imagination, let alone doubt or discussion.

I have learned to create my own experience of God, a real, continually creative force, of which each of us is only a fragment, an energy that surpasses such concepts as good and evil, that operates in terms of equilibrium.

Hilólómbi means "the oldest of the old" and is symbolic of

God. The difference between God and man is that man is only a part of the total energy. The part contains all properties of the whole but can express this only in approximate terms. Man is handicapped by all kinds of petty limitations. For me, evolution means that we become increasingly better at reproducing the greatness that produced us. To do that, you must be able to draw upon the accumulated knowledge, a knowledge that reveals itself during initiation. During ritual initiations, various masks are used to promote insight into the world, an understanding of the culture within us.

The ritual masks serve to obscure the personality and its pettiness, and to spur us on to achieve something greater. I think if you can understand that, you can have some insight into the basic principles of traditional African culture. You will also be better able to understand why the glorification of the personality in Africa has come at the cost of so many other things, and why it has been so fatal for us.

Ki-Yi means "the highest knowledge." *Ki-Yi Mbock* is the name of an extremely old Bassa initiation ritual that prepared the people to overcome a serious crisis. The last time this traditional rite was used was during the Ambassa War, which resulted in the migration of the Bassas during the thirteenth and fourteenth centuries. At that time, the Bassas came down from western Nigeria to the coastal region of what is now Cameroon.

Oral tradition tells us that a certain Ki-Yi was responsible for diplomatic relations during that war. His descendants and numerous followers saw to it that blood was not shed during the exodus. My aunt and teacher, Kelbe Ngoen, the great Aede of Nding, of Koo and Mbee, female initiates of the Bassa, passed this knowledge along to me as a part of the oral tradition. She thought it was time to breathe new life into the *Ki-Yi Mbock*: to appreciate *Ki-Yi* as a concept of accumulated knowledge that can offer a solution to crisis. "Ki-Yi Mbock" is the name of my theater group.

I truly believe that traditional ritual retains its power as long as it is adapted to the times and the people. The content of the rituals does not become obsolete, the form does. That's why the form of the ritual must always grow along with the people, adapt itself to their own specific initiation needs. Social life, after all, is based on rituals. The ritual is a communication code from yourself to yourself (initiation into the discovery of your inner being) and from yourself to the other (initiation into the operations of society). Without rituals, a society cannot function. How can we be thoughtful of others without the unwritten laws of civility? These rules of etiquette are rituals. But they must evolve along with the understanding and the sensitivity of those who implement them; otherwise they become fossilized.

To understand the experience of ritual theater, you must draw a distinction between ritual, which you experience at a realistic level, and ritual theater, which is an art form, a re-creation, a re-adaptation, an investigation of that experienced—or even a critique of it.

Ritual theater does not pretend to be a school or a movement, nor does it want to be a museum full of abandoned and forgotten relics or a place where a few magic rituals are unveiled. Our theater is ritual because it takes its inspiration from certain aspects of the old ritual ideology and its communication mechanisms.

During a ritual performance, every member of the audience has the opportunity to react at his or her own level: emotionally, intellectually, or physically. He is therefore also responsible for the way things go: Every member of the audience becomes, by definition, a participant. Every ritual results in a consensus, for which everyone shares responsibility. It has often happened that a performance has bogged down because there was someone who refused to go along, who crossed his legs or refused to clap along. It is precisely that shared responsibility that allows a common problem to be solved, questions to be answered, deeds to be condemned, which allows cursing, blessing, or healing. To achieve this effective communality, communication mechanisms must be put in motion that are aimed at the senses, the emotions, the psyche, and the intellect in order to release the creative process in everyone. That is why ritual, whether religious or profane, is largely initiatory.

As for communication mechanisms, we are talking about the use of different words—the spoken word, the word of gesture, the musical word, the word symbolized by color, objects—at the various levels of language: ordinary language, the psychodramatic, therapeutic, poetic invocatory language or esoteric language. It seems that the initiation takes place during the ritual theater performance. Each symbol takes its meaning from the mise-en-scène, during the actors' performance, and not by definition within the framework of a given culture.

The members of our audience cannot muffle themselves away in the margin of what is happening onstage. The important thing is the theater, which ruptures logic and displays the difference between what people say and what they do. It is a form of theater that lends itself more to long-term examination than to passive, on-the-spot consumption.

A ritual is based on the dividing line between personal interest and community responsibility. The ritual makes it possible to formulate certain problems and solve them in communal agreement. Traditionally, a ritual always follows on the heels of a situation of imbalance. In the entire history of Africa there has never been a time of such utter imbalance as that in which we live today. In a certain sense, my theater has therapeutic value. Anything that reduces ignorance and lack of understanding and promotes greater awareness is, in the long run, therapeutic. I have seen how the traditional rituals have stimulated the personal involvement and therefore the responsibility of the participants as well. I have noticed how important the spoken word can be.

Speech is the giving of form to thought, for its fulfillment through an act. In my native language we say: "Speech is the eldest daughter of thought." But there is a great difference between speech and the verb. The verb is a form of speech in which the act lies enclosed. There is virginal and sterile speech. The verb is speech that is pregnant with the act and will necessarily bear that act.

Rituals are based on active words. Ritual speech adapts itself constantly. That is why it is so important that the people who serve society through rituals be initiated. The power of the word depends upon the good will and faithfulness of the people who speak it. Otherwise speech is only sound, noise without content.

In political circumstances such as ours, as I have sketched them, the creativity of the people has been nipped in the bud, because they have had to submit to everything without the possibility of having it put up for discussion. What could we do against the words the West forced us to swallow, while our own armies had their weapons pointed at us? In such a situation words become a mask, intended to obscure deeper feelings. In a situation like that, it is very important to see and hear nothing, that is, if one means to survive and avoid taking a thrashing in the short term. After all, hearing and seeing generate emotions that can lead to questions about the point of living. Without those questions, active living is replaced by an instinctive urge to survive.

When I was a child, I hated being a girl. The men were the only ones who did important, special things. I wanted to find that "word of power" that men seemed to possess. Later I discovered what an important role women play in everything. I gradually became reconciled to being a woman. That came late.

I am still looking for the "word of power" everywhere: in my texts, in my paintings, in my performances and my songs. I am also looking for this "word of power" in my private life, albeit with the exaggerated caution of feet that have already felt the serpent's bite.

I no longer believe in words very much, not even when they are spoken by people who are true to themselves. But I do believe in great feelings that eradicate all barriers, all force, all fears, and that cause us to perform increasingly better deeds.

Translated from the Dutch
by Sam Garrett

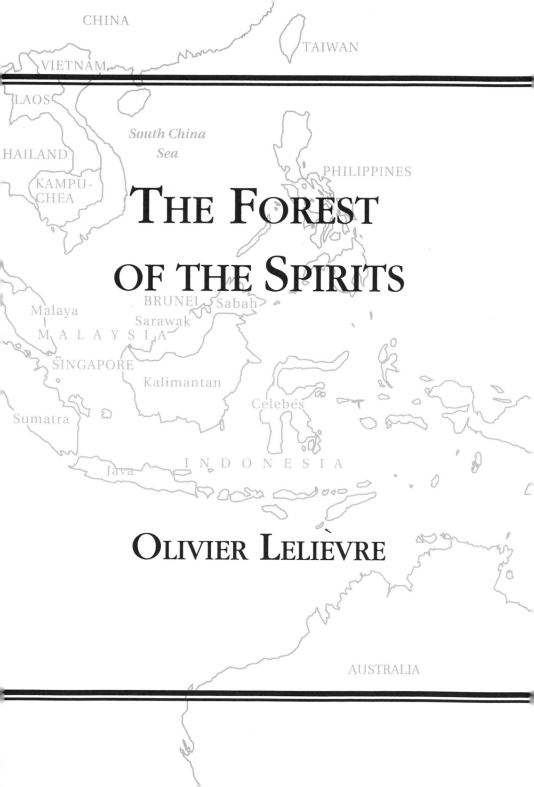

THE FOREST
OF THE SPIRITS

OLIVIER LELIÈVRE

Olivier Lelièvre at left.

Olivier Lelièvre is a photographer, an ethnographer, and a member of the Geographic Society of France. He has studied Indochina and Southeast Asia extensively.

Mr. Lelièvre traveled to Borneo on numerous occasions where he lived among the Punan of central Borneo and the Kenya of Southeast Asia. Similarly, between 1989 and 1990 he spent six months in Siberut, Indonesia, with the Mentawaï.

Mr. Lelièvre is the author of *Balan Tribulations à Bornéo*. The following selection is excerpted from his book *Mentawaï : La Forêt des Esprits*.

Biligo Teo Kani is a small man with bow legs and an arched back that make his gait appear odd. He does not have a beautiful body, nor does he share the particularly graceful bearing characteristic of his people, the Mentawaï. And yet this little man who wears a weather-beaten grass skirt and tattoos, and often a mirthful twinkle in his eyes, is respected by all.

Biligo is a *sikerei*, or shaman, one of those who have the power to communicate with souls, ancestors, and spirits. This particular skill allows him to drive evil spirits from a sick person's body and bring back his stray soul. To achieve this feat, Biligo must remember many chants and prayers, repeating them often when he is alone in order not to forget them. He also knows the *Arat Sabulugan*, the group of laws and customs that determine the order of the universe, which were passed on to him by his ancestors. Biligo is experienced in making use of plants and roots, intermediaries between the supernatural and the human worlds. He is particularly partial to the lianas*, symbols of longevity that are also used to spread harmony among the members of his clan.

As a shaman, Biligo is often requested to participate in ceremonies such as the healing of a sick person, the dedication of a new house, or the induction of a new *sikerei*. He is therefore at the center of the social and religious preoccupations of his brethren. In contrast with a great number of his colleagues, however, he gains no personal glory from all his activities, for the ancestors and the spirits *chose* him for this job. He fulfills his duties to the best of his ability to preserve the peace and harmony vital to human happiness. His occupations do not give him any special

---

*lianas—climbing plants or vines.

privileges; in his daily life, he must carry out the same tasks as all of the other Mentawaï. In recent days, however, his heart has not been in them.

A few weeks ago, the fragile souls of his two youngest children wandered a little too far and got lost. While they were sick, Biligo had done everything to coax back their souls, to please them and to show them how beautiful life on earth could be. Never before had he been armed with so many flowers and croton leaves. Never had he danced with such vigor, never pleaded with the spirits with such fervor to allow his children to return. He and his *sikerei* friends had danced all night long, until they were completely exhausted. They had danced, they had laughed, they had eaten. But then, and despite everything, his children had left him a few days later. What had he done to cause their souls to go toward their ancestors like that, leaving him and his wife as emptyhanded as when they had begun? He did not know and could not find any answers. In grief, Biligo sat in a dark corner of his kitchen. To his lips he lifted his *pipiau*, or "companion of tears," a flute reserved for times of sorrow, and started to play a slow and repetitive melody that rose toward the skies, toward the souls of his two children.

Biligo sits bowed with pain. For him the real world no longer exists. Perhaps he is trying to imagine his children's life among the souls of the clan's ancestors, so high above earth and beneath the celestial arch.

Within his eyes, clouded with tears, there is a great ocean, the original one that gave birth to the universe, to the world as well as to the sky. Biligo's island, Siberut, is at the center of this ocean. All around it are other isles; Biligo knows this even if he has not seen them.

To the East, in that place where the universe was born, is Manua, the celestial land. One day, Manua began to grow like a bamboo shoot, both sturdy and pliant; then it bent

itself into the dome that covers the human world. At the foot of Manua, to the East, lived White Men who watered the bamboo shoot with oil so that the world could continue to grow. Later, when the dome was completed, the sun and moon appeared and set out traveling along the celestial arch toward the West.

A great crocodile lived where the twilight replaced the night. The first time that it saw the two stars coming, the crocodile wanted to eat them. But it did not take into account all the Red Men who lived in that region of the universe. As the crocodile watched the drama unfold, the Red Men prepared little balls of taro*, a bulb that is eaten often on Siberut. As soon as the crocodile opened its mouth, they threw the taro into it. The animal swallowed this food, thus saving the sun and the moon, who continued on their way toward the West. Then they turned and went beneath the world so that they could reappear on the other side the next morning and all the subsequent mornings.

In the beginning, the celestial arch was so close to the earth that the sun burned women and children when they bathed in the river. To move the sky back, the men took up their bows and fired their arrows at the sky. They pierced it with millions of tiny holes, which became stars. Under this pelting of arrows, the dome retreated to its present position.

Biligo had heard this story over and over during his childhood. His friends, however related a different story regarding the origin of stars. As he contemplated his friends, Biligo could not keep from smiling. Those people surely must be mistaken; how could his own ancestors have passed on tall tales?

According to Mentawaï legends, the stars are the children of the moon. The sun had children too, but the heat from all those "little suns" had been unbearable. The

---

*taro—stemless plant found in tropical regions.

moon, out of pity for humans, spread the red juice from coconut shells all over her lips so that they would appear bloody. Then she found the sun and told him that she had just eaten her children. The sun, following the moon's example, ate his own offspring; but when night fell, the stars reappeared. The sun understood that he had been tricked. He became very angry and cut the moon into pieces with a giant knife. That is why, to this very day, we sometimes see the moon in quarters.

The moon, to avenge herself, procured a machete and tried in vain to slice up her enemy. This is how the Mentawaï explain the sun's rays, its vague shape, and the fact that, since that distant time, you never see these two great stars together.

Moreover, toward the end of each month the moon falls ill, becoming thinner by the day. Finally she strays from her regular path so that she may enter the "garden of the yellow roots," where she dies. Later, she is resurrected and starts her cycle all over again.

Above the human world and under the celestial arch is the village where live the spirits, the *sikamanua*. Biligo does not know how these beings appeared, but he is certain that they have a human shape.

A wonderful girl, the Daughter of the Sky, lives here. One day, long ago, she decided to marry a human. From their union, a long vine was created to allow mortals to climb up to the Laggai Sabeu, the ancestors' village. Nonetheless, danger still hovered over humanity. The Daughter of the Sky has a brother named Kangut who lives on the moon. He has never accepted his sister's marriage to a human. To prevent his brother-in-law and those like him from regaining paradise, Kangut knotted a long rope that was meant to catch them. Kangut's wife, who hid beneath the moon and did not understand her husband's point of view, cut the knotted rope when it became too long. Since then, Kangut has spent all of his time trying to make it longer.

Biligo, lost in his thoughts, imagines his two children in this village paradise, so far from him, too far from him. Why do humans have to be mortal? Erupting from the deepest part of his memory, another Mentawaï myth offers an answer.

In the beginning of time, humans were immortal. But one day Pageta Sabau, a shaman with very potent magical powers, decided to put them to a test. He asked them to choose between two dishes. The first one consisted of bananas and fish; the second, of yams and shrimp. The humans made the wrong choice, selecting the first dish, and accordingly had to die like the banana tree, which bears fruit only once. Had they chosen the second dish, they would still be immortal like the young yams, which can be replanted and give off new tubers.

Further, death was not really final in the beginning. Pageta Sabbau could bring the deceased back to life by walking on their corpses. One day, despite his warnings, the humans invited him to their home. The all-too-brutal meeting of their respective souls caused the shaman's death and his transformation into a spirit. Some young men who also wanted to become *sikerei*, and who were bent on completing their education with Pageta Sabbau, came upon the festivities. They did not know he had become a spirit, and what they saw shocked them: They saw their master in double. They were terrified and thought they were in the presence of an evil spirit. Pageta Sabbau, deeply hurt that he could be confused with evil beings, created a violent wind to strike the students on their way home. Petrified, they retreated and came upon a beach where they could contemplate their dead relatives. Pageta Sabbau announced to them that, given their behavior, they would never see their ancestors again. He then changed the beach into a dizzying cliff. That is why, since then, death is final and inevitable.

The *sikamanua* and the ancestors who share the skies are enemies of the inhabitants of the underworld, the Kabaga. Teteu, the earthquake spirit, is the most important of these. In the beginning, Teteu was a human being, an orphaned boy who lived with his sister at the home of their father's brother. One day, the little family and some neighbors went into the forest to pick vegetables and plants. Teteu could find only roots and rotten fruit. As soon as Teteu's family began to eat them, however, the roots and rotten fruit became delicious. Not understanding this miracle, his companions became frightened and cast off the young boy and his sister. A large river separated the village from the plantations. When it was time to go home, the children were placed in a canoe that they could not handle. Teteu and his sister seemed certain to be drowned, but one of the water spirits, who had the shape of a crocodile, took pity on them. She told them that she was their father's sister and carried them onto the shore. Later she taught Teteu how to build an *uma*—a large communal house typical of Mentawaï lodgings—as well as the taboos one had to respect and the rituals one had to perform before one could move into the *uma*.

Teteu, with the crocodile's help, went straight to work. The house that he started to build was so beautiful that the other men were jealous. They tricked him into climbing into the hole where the main pilotis* were going to be put. As soon as he was inside, they killed him with a volley of arrows, and Teteu became a spirit within the earth. When the *uma* had been completed and the dedication ceremony was about to begin, he released an earthquake that destroyed the *uma* along with many victims.

The cultural roots of the Mentawaï go back to the Neolithic age, over 3,000 years ago. They came from the north, via

---

*piloti—column supporting a building above open ground level.

Malaysia, Sumatra, and Nias. Under pressure from more aggressive populations, they and other peoples settled over the entire Indonesian archipelago, in a series of waves. These newcomers, including the Dayak of Borneo and the Toradjas of Sulawesi, dispersed and finally developed into autonomous cultures on each of the islands.

In contrast to most Indonesian populations, the Mentawaï are unfamiliar with rice cultivation, metalworking, weaving, and pottery. Their staple food is sago*, but they also cultivate coconut and banana trees as well as yams. Livestock is limited to pigs and chickens. Daily routines are augmented by hunting (with bows or traps) and fishing.

The Mentawaï have remained isolated and therefore did not feel the influence of other societies until the beginning of the twentieth century, when the Dutch allowed missionaries to proselytize the local populations. To escape these foreigners, several groups fled, taking refuge in the remotest parts of the island. That is where one can still find the last representatives of this culture, which springs from the earliest history of humankind.

Biligo Teo Kani remembers well the time when he constructed his own *uma*. Life was so nice then! He had chosen to leave the home he shared with his parents, his uncles, his brothers and their families, and his unmarried sisters. There were too many people under one roof. Even when the hunt had been good, everyone received only small amounts of meat when it had been divided up. Biligo, like all the Mentawaï, could not conceive of life outside his community. He therefore persuaded one of his brothers to follow him with his wife and children. He had just gotten married himself and was already dreaming of the many children he would soon have.

---

*sago—a starchy foodstuff derived from the soft interior of the trunk of palm trees, used in making puddings.

Helped by his family and friends, Biligo undertook building his *uma*—a long and difficult job. He first had to cut large trees in the forest to make the pilotis and master beams; then he cut dozens of pieces of wood for the floors and walls of the two enclosed rooms. At that time, the *sasareu*, or men of the distant road (in fact, the merchants coming from Sumatra), had not yet imported nails. He had to make thousands of pegs to fasten his structure. As for the women, they collected hundreds of sago palm branches for the roof. When the house was finished, Biligo killed many of his pigs and organized a great celebration. The entire family participated. They brought numerous gifts, and his father gave him a plot of land with beautiful sago palms.

Sitting in front of a mosquito net, Biligo looks at his *uma*, illuminated by the firelight from the kitchen where his wife is making sago flour. It is still central to his thoughts and in a symbolic manner sums up his entire universe: The space between the pilotis represents the inner world; the space underground represents Teteu's realm; the *uma*'s floor symbolizes the intermediate world where his dead relatives live; and the roof represents Manua, the celestial arch, that is to say, the divine world.

Glancing to the door, he notices the front part of the veranda where a few friends, sitting on benches weathered by time, are involved in a lively discussion. This room, the *laikobat*, has an external view. The *laikobat* is without doubt the pleasantest part of the house. It is airy, and one can perform daily tasks while keeping an eye on activities outside.

Three big doors, which are rarely closed, give access to the main room of the *uma*. This room, the *puligat*, is walled by planks of wood on each side and is pierced by two small window-like openings that admit diffuse light. It is the room where all social and ritual activities take place. In the middle of it, in front of the space reserved for dancing, stands the hearth, which is used for cooking meat during ritual meals.

Above the hearth, a beam cuts across the width of the room. Here are hung all the hunting trophies of the men living in the *uma*. The skulls of monkeys, deer, and wild pigs look out at the exterior of the house. They have been meticulously painted and decorated throughout the years. Knotted palm leaves, symbolizing the forest, and bird sculptures complete the harmonious setting. Like those of any living creature, the souls of these dead animals can separate themselves from their bodies to wander and live independently. The purpose of the decoration is to make the animal spirits comfortable in the house so that they will remain with their skulls. Before going off to hunt, Biligo never forgets to offer a sacrifice to these trophies so that they will invite the souls of the animals in the forest to join them. In this way, those who hear the invitation will perhaps allow themselves to be killed by the hunters.

The skulls of pigs sacrificed during communal ceremonies are hung on the partitions that separate the veranda from the main room. In contrast with the other skulls, their gaze is directed toward the interior of the *uma* because, in this instance, they are pets. The animal souls that live in this spot must watch over the successful breeding of Biligo's domesticated pigs. They are also supposed to lure them so that they will accept being killed when the time comes.

Above the entrance to the last room is the *jaraik*. The soft lines and well-balanced shape of this wooden sculpture seem directly inspired by the idea of a harmonious world that governs the lives of the Mentawaï. This sculpture is difficult to make and is now very rare. It constitutes a barrier that wards off evil forces. At the center of the *jaraik*, a skull of a fat monkey is meant to insure good hunts to each of the families in the *uma*.

The last room, where Biligo lives, which is called the *rapo* or *abu*, is where the women usually work. The families share two foyers. They are located beneath the stocks of wood at the end of this kitchen, where the heavy smell of smoke and intimacy can be felt.

To the right of the entrance, on a piloti considered to be one of the most important ones in the house and next to the gongs, hangs the main fetish of the house: the *bakkat katsaila*, a bouquet made of various plants, roots, and lianas that are intermediaries between the natural and supernatural worlds. Their function is to ward off evil and attract good. There is a plant that insures abundance; one that wards off evil spirits; one that insures peace among members of the group; and the croton, the symbol of gratitude. The *bakkat katsaila* possesses its own soul (*kina*), which is the protective spirit of the *uma* and which insures the happiness of all the group members.

Biligo, besides his duties as a *sikerei*, is also a *rimata*, a guardian of the traditions of the house and the representative of his people to the clans. He is the one who organizes ceremonies, makes sure they go well, and interprets supernatural signs. Large communal festivals bring all the groups of the *uma* together and express the united and equal nature of the group as a whole. The house has no ruler, and all members are equal. Decisions are taken collectively, and everyone shares responsibility for the most important tasks. During the daily work schedule, many activities are carried out collectively. In this way, the members of the house feel united by strong links of solidarity and cooperation, which are considered essential by the Mentawaï.

Biligo would not leave his *uma* for anything in the world, and most people would agree with his attitude. When his eldest daughter got married, she followed her husband to one of the modern villages built by the authorities to gather populations who have traditionally lived in the forest. Biligo visits there on occasion, and he wonders how she can live in these ready-made buildings, all stan-

Olivier Lelièvre

dardized, and so small and hot with their zinc roofs. How can they cultivate the tiny plots of land given to those who agree to live in these complexes? The men in the village confirm that these modern villages allow the Mentawaï to adapt to the modern world more easily. Schools, clinics, mosques, and churches are all available to the inhabitants. The men learn to cultivate rice by burning the earth and refertilizing it, which had been unknown to them previously. Biligo is certain: He would never agree to live there. Why would he want to learn how to cultivate rice when the sago palm and the taro are bountiful and the forest provides for all his needs? How could he maintain his pigs when it is forbidden to keep them, for reasons of hygiene, near the house? And then Biligo does not really understand the purpose of schools, or clinics, or those strange places of worship, since until now everything had gone smoothly without them. A number of Biligo's friends did go to live in the modern villages. Some of them more or less adapted to the new existence, but others returned to the forest to continue to live according to the traditions established by their ancestors.

Biligo starts to come out of his daydream. Around him, the women are busy preparing the evening meal in the shadows of early evening. Sitting beneath the door frame, one of them sifts the flour to make it finer. A little farther away, his wife lets a little sago flour fall from her fingers into the cavities of the long palm leaf. With the confidence of gestures that have been repeated a million times before, she closes each leaf around the sago and places it on the fire.

A few minutes later, dinner is ready. All the families come and make themselves comfortable in a corner of the room, around a cauldron of steamy food, with sago shoots and a little oil lamp. All around, dogs try to get near the treats, but the men are always there to shoo them gently away. They too have souls, and so it would be wrong to offend them.

98

Once dinner is eaten, everybody gathers on the veranda to chat and smoke a few local cigarettes. Biligo, as he always does, tidies up and checks the tools he will need the next day when he cultivates the sago palms in his garden. Then he joins his friends in enjoying a sweet moment of laziness.

The evening goes by slowly. Little by little, the women go off to bed with their children under the mosquito nets in the kitchen. The men stay among themselves in the main room of the *uma*. Later, when everyone is asleep, they will return to their mates to share a few tender moments; then they will go back to their own mosquito nets. Their souls might feel neglected after too much sexual activity.

The adolescents are in no rush to stretch out under their nets. They prefer to disappear discreetly to visit their friends or fiancés in the surrounding cabins. Sexual relations between young people are not forbidden but—out of a sense of modesty, no doubt—they are circumspect. As he listens to their laughter and the rhythm of their voices, Biligo smiles a dreamy smile.

Translated from the French by Peter Schulman

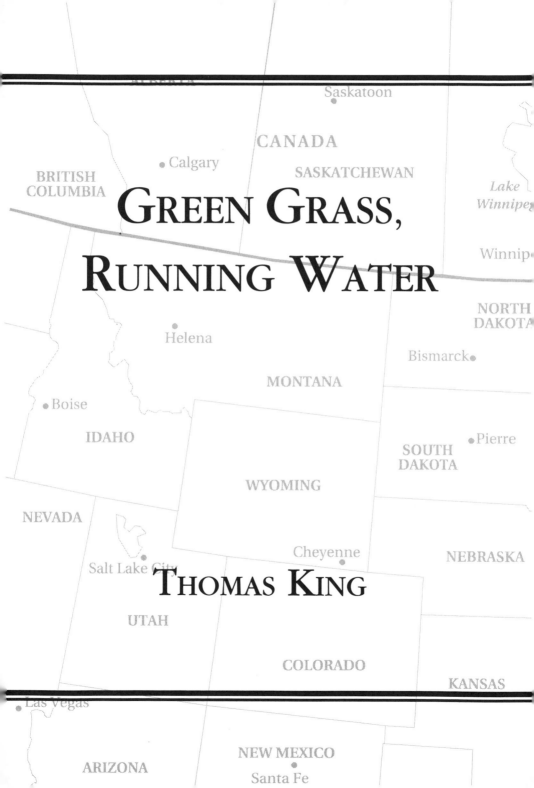

GREEN GRASS,
RUNNING WATER

THOMAS KING

© Timothy Francisco

T homas King was born in Sacramento, California. He holds a Ph.D. in American studies from the University of Utah.

Dr. King is the author of *Medicine River*, for which he received the Alberta Writers Guild Best Novel Award in 1990 and the Josephine Miles/Oakland PEN Award in 1991, and of *A Coyote Columbus Story.* He edited *All My Relations: An Anthology of Short Fiction by Native Writers in Canada* and coedited *The Native in Literature.* Dr. King received the National Magazine Award silver medal for his short story "Borders," published in *Saturday Night* magazine. His fiction and nonfiction have also been published in the *Malabat Review, Hungry Mind Review,* and *American Indian Quarterly,* among others.

Dr. King is an associate professor of American Studies and Chairman of the American Indian Studies Department at the University of Minnesota. He lives in St. Paul, Minnesota.

The following is an excerpt from his forthcoming novel *Green Grass, Running Water,* to be published in March 1993 by Houghton Mifflin.

Eli Stands Alone stood at the window of the cabin and watched the water slide past the porch. It was getting higher, but they had done that before, open the gates just a little and let the stream come up over the sides of the channel and wash against the logs. A lot of trouble for nothing.

He took his cup of coffee out on the porch and sat down in the easy chair. Two hundred yards away, he could see the dam, an immense porcelain wall, white and glistening in the late morning light.

Eli could also see Cliff Sifton walking down the stream bed; he waved, and Cliff waved back.

"You want some coffee?" Eli shouted, though he knew Cliff couldn't hear him above the rush of the water. Cliff raised his walking stick and shouted back, but Eli couldn't hear him either.

Eli brought the coffee pot out and put it out on the table. The water was still rising, and Cliff was having difficulty wading through the thigh-deep, gray-green water as it tumbled over the granite riprap. The water buffeted Cliff's legs, and Eli could see the man rocking and balancing as he stepped from rock to rock, picking his way across the stream.

"Guess they're mad as hell about the injunction," Eli said.

"Guess you're right," said Cliff, making the porch and looking at the coffee pot. "Brewed or instant?"

"Always make brewed. You know that. You always ask me that, and it's always brewed."

"That one time it was instant."

"You guys flooded me in for two weeks. What'd you expect? Besides, that was seven years ago."

"Always pays to ask." Cliff pulled a package out of his

knapsack. "Here," he said. "Where do you want it?"

Cliff poured a cup of coffee and leaned his stick against the porch railing. "How you think the fishing is going to be this year?"

"Should be good. Be better if your dam wasn't there."

"Not my dam, Eli. And you know it." Cliff sat on the railing and squinted at the sun.

Eli settled in the chair. "What do you figure? Now or later?"

"Now, probably," said Cliff. "No sense in wasting good coffee and a beautiful day. You know, we haven't had any wind for almost a week."

"Weather pattern," said Eli. "It'll change."

"I know it'll change. I just want to enjoy another day without that damn wind."

Eli leaned over the arm of his chair and watched the water. "Looks like it's going down."

"Just before I left, I told them to back off."

"Came pretty close this time."

"We know our business."

"So ask the question."

Cliff put his coffee cup down and pulled a white card out of his jacket pocket. He looked out over the stream, cleared his throat, and began to read.

Eli's mother died while he was teaching in Toronto. No one told him about her death until his sister called.

"Mom died," Norma said.

"When?"

"Couple of weeks ago."

"What? Why didn't you phone me?"

"Last time we saw you was twenty years ago."

"Norma..."

"Haven't phoned in four or five years, either."

"It hasn't been that long."

"Thought you might have died."

"I could have helped," Eli said.

"Didn't need you. Camelot and I took care of everything. I was going to call, but then I forgot. I remembered today, so I called."

"I could have helped," Eli said.

"You can help now," said Norma.

There was the matter of their mother's house, Norma told him. No one could live in it because it was right in the middle of the proposed spillway for the Grand Baleen Dam, but Norma thought Eli might want to see the place or take a picture of it before it was flooded or torn down or whatever they did to things like that that were in the way of progress. There was even some furniture in the house that Eli could have if he wanted.

"You were born there before you went off and became white," Norma told him, "so I thought it might be of sentimental value. I hear if you're a famous enough white guy, the government will buy the house where you were born and turn it into one of those tourist things."

Eli hung up before Norma could really get rolling. The next day he caught a plane to Blossom, hired a car at the airport, and drove all the way to the reserve without stopping.

It was morning when he walked out of the trees and across the meadow to his mother's house. Off to the west he could see bulldozers and semi-trucks and a couple of portable offices.

His mother had built the house. Log by log. Had dragged each one out of the small stand of timber behind the house, barked them, hewn them, and set them. He and Norma had been too young to help, and Camelot was only a baby then. So they looked after their sister while their mother coaxed the trees into place.

Cliff Sifton had come down from the dam site that day and walked the length of the meadow, his walking stick stabbing at the ground. He had stood at the bottom of the porch and looked up at Eli.

"Morning," he said, shading his eyes. "Saw you drive up."

"Morning," Eli repeated.

"You must be Eli Stands Alone."

"That's right."

"Your sister says you teach in Toronto. At the University?"

"That's right."

"What do you teach?"

"Literature."

"Don't suppose you have any coffee?"

Eli couldn't put a name to it, but he didn't like Cliff. He didn't want to make him any coffee. And he didn't want the man on his mother's porch.

"Looks like you're thinking about building a dam?"

"That's right," said Cliff. "She's going to be a beauty."

"This is my mother's house."

"Your sister said you might want some things out of it before we tear it down."

"She built it herself, log by log."

"If there are any big pieces, sing out, and I'll send some of the boys to give you a hand."

Eli ran his hands along the railing, feeling for the carvings that he and Norma had cut into the wood. In the distance, he could hear a diesel motor turn over.

"Nobody's going to tear down this house."

"Construction starts in a month."

"Nobody's going to tear down this house."

Cliff looked at Eli, and he looked back at the bulldozers and the semis and the portable offices. "Nothing personal," he said, smiling and extending his hand.

Eli took Cliff's hand and held it for a second with just the fingers, the way you would hold something fragile or dangerous. "Okay," he said, "nothing personal."

*   *   *

Eli shielded his eyes. From where he sat on the porch, he imagined he could see the cracks that were developing near the base of the dam. Stress fractures they called them, common enough in any dam, but troublesome nonetheless, especially given the relatively young age of the concrete. Of more concern was the slumping that had been discovered along the north end of the dam.

"It's a beauty, isn't it?" said Cliff Sifton, swirling the remains of the coffee around in the cup. "You got a great view of it."

"View was better before you built it."

"You always say that, Eli, as if it's going to go away. But it's not."

"Reminds me of a toilet."

"You always say that, too."

"Hear they found some more cracks in the dam."

"All dams do that."

"Hear they think the earth is moving under the dam."

"You always get cracks in dams."

"So they say."

The clouds to the northwest were filling up the sky. They had been slowly organizing and gathering all day. Eli turned his face into the wind. Rain.

Cliff set his coffee cup on the railing. "You know, I always thought Indians were elegant speakers."

"Storm's coming."

"But all you ever say is no. I come by every day and read that thing those lawyers thought up about voluntarily extinguishing your right to this house and the land it sits on, and all you ever say is no."

"Be here by tonight."

"I mean, no isn't exactly elegant now, is it?"

"Maybe get some hail, too."

"It's hard work walking down here every day, and it would help if sometime you would tell me why."

*   *   *

Every July, when Eli was growing up, his mother would close the cabin and move the family to the Sun Dance. Eli would help the other men set up the teepee and then he and Norma and Camelot would run with the kids in the camp. They would ride the horses and chase each other across the prairies, their freedom only interrupted by the ceremonies.

Best of all, Eli liked the men's dancing. The women would dance for four days, and then there would be a day of rest and the men would begin. Each afternoon, toward evening, the Horn Society would come out of the lodge and dance. Just before the sun set, one of the dancers would pick up a rifle and lead the other men to the east end of the camp where the children waited. Eli and the rest of the children would stand in a pack and wave pieces of scrap paper at the dancers as the men attacked and fell back, surged forward and retreated, until finally, after several of these mock forays, the lead dancer would breach the fortress of children and fire the rifle and all the children would fall down in a heap, laughing, full of fear and pleasure, the pieces of paper scattering across the land.

Then the dancers would gather up the food that was piled around the flagpole—bread, macaroni, canned soup, sardines, instant noodles—and pass it out to the people. Later, after the camp settled in, Eli and Norma and Camelot would lie on their backs and watch the stars as they appeared among the teepee poles through the opening in the top of the tent.

And each morning, because the sun returned and the people remembered, it would begin again.

"Look, it's not my idea," Cliff raised his arms in surrender. "It's all those lawyers and the injunctions and that barrel load of crap about Native rights."

"Treaty rights, Cliff."

"Almost as bad as French rights. Damn sure wish the

government would give me some of that."

"Government didn't give us anything, Cliff. We paid for them. Paid for them two or three times."

"And so because the government felt generous back in the last ice age and made promises it never intended to keep, I have to come by every morning and ask the same stupid question."

"And I say no."

"You know you're going to say no, and I know you're going to say no. Hell, the whole damn world knows you're going to say no."

"So why come?"

Cliff looked at Eli, and both men began to chuckle. "Because you make the best damn coffee. And because I like the walk."

"Answer will be the same tomorrow."

Every year or so, a tourist would wander into the camp. Sometimes they were invited. Other times they just saw the camp from the road and were curious. Most of the time, they were friendly, and no one seemed to mind them. Occasionally there was trouble.

When Eli was fourteen, a station wagon with British Columbia plates pulled off the road and into the camp just as the men were finishing their second day of dancing. Before anyone realized what was happening, the man climbed on top of the car and began taking pictures.

Eli saw the man and told his uncle Orville, who quickly gathered up his two brothers and their sons and descended on the car. The guy must have seen the men coming, because he slid off the car, climbed into the driver's seat, rolled up all the windows, and locked all the doors.

The men surrounded the station wagon. Orville motioned for the man inside to roll down his window. There was a woman sitting in the passenger seat and a little girl and a baby in the back. Orville tapped on the glass, and the man just smiled and nodded his head.

Things stayed like that for quite a while. The dancers finished, and, as word went around, a large part of the camp moved in on the car. The baby in the car began to cry. Finally the man stopped smiling and began to wave at Orville, motioning for him and the rest of the people to get out of the way.

"Roll down your window," Orville said, his voice low and controlled.

Instead the man started his engine, revved it, as if he were going to drive right through the people. As soon as the man started the car, Orville's brother Leroy went to his truck and grabbed his rifle off the rack. He walked to the front of the van and held the gun over his head. The man in the car looked at Leroy for a moment, yelled something at his wife, and turned off the engine.

Then he rolled the window down just a crack. "What's the problem?"

"This is our Sun Dance, you know."

"No," said the man. "I didn't know. I thought it was a powwow or something."

"No," said Orville. "It isn't a powwow. It's our Sun Dance."

"Well, I didn't know that."

"You can't take pictures of the Sun Dance."

"Well, I didn't know that."

"Now you know. So I have to ask you for the pictures you took."

The man looked over at his wife, who nodded her head ever so slightly. "Well," he said, "I didn't take any pictures."

"You got a camera," Orville said.

"We're on vacation," said the man. "I was going to take some pictures of your little powwow, but I didn't."

Orville looked at Leroy, who was still standing in front of the van, the rifle cradled in his arms. "Is that so?"

"Yes," said the man. "That's the truth. Take it or leave it."

Orville put his hand on Eli's shoulder. "My nephew here says he saw you taking pictures."

The man's wife suddenly leaned over and grabbed her husband's arm. "Give them the pictures, Bill! For God's sake, just give them the pictures!"

The man turned, shook her arm off, and pushed her against the door. He sat there a moment, looking at the dash, his hands squeezing the wheel. "I got pictures of my family on that roll," he said to Orville. "Tell you what. When I get them developed, if there happen to be any pictures of this thing, I'll send them to you along with the negatives."

Orville took out a handkerchief and blew his nose. "No," he said very slowly. "That's not the way it's going to work. I think it's best if you give us the film and my brother will get it developed. We'll send you the pictures that are yours."

"There are some very important pictures on that roll."

"Yes, there are," said Orville.

Eli had never seen someone so angry. It was hot in the car and the man was sweating, but it wasn't from the heat. Eli could see the muscles on the man's neck, could hear the violent, exaggerated motions with which he unloaded the camera and passed the film through the window to Orville.

Cliff pushed off the railing and snapped to attention, lowering his voice to a deep growl. "I am required by law to respectfully request that you relinquish your claim to this house and the land on which it sits and that title to this property be properly vested with the Province of Alberta."

Cliff quickly sat down in the chair next to Eli and smiled up at the character he had just created.

"No," Cliff said, imitating as best he could Eli's soft voice.

Eli laughed and shook his head. "That's pretty good, Cliff. Real soon you'll be able to do it all by yourself. You won't need me at all."

Cliff stayed in the chair. "You know what the problem is? This country doesn't have an Indian policy. Nobody knows what the hell anyone else is doing."

"Got the treaties."

"Hell, Eli, those treaties aren't worth a damn. Government only made them for convenience. Who'd of guessed that there'd still be Indians kicking around in the twentieth century."

"One of life's little embarrassments."

"Besides, you guys aren't real Indians anyway. I mean, you drive cars, watch television, go to hockey games. Look at you. You're a university professor."

"That's my profession. Being Indian isn't a profession."

"And you speak as good English as me."

"Better. And I speak Blackfoot, too. My sister Norma speaks Blackfoot. So do my niece and nephew."

"That's what I mean. Latisha runs a restaurant and Lionel sells televisions. Not exactly traditionalists, are they?"

"It's not exactly the nineteenth century, either."

"Damn it. That's my point. You can't live in the past. My dam is part of the twentieth century. Your house is part of the nineteenth."

"Maybe I should look into putting it on the historical register."

Cliff rubbed his hands on his pants. "You know, when I was in high school, I read a story about a guy just like you who didn't want to do anything to improve his life. He just sat on a stool in some dark room and said 'I would prefer not to.' That's all he said."

"Bartleby the Scrivener."

"What?"

"Bartleby the Scrivener. One of Herman Melville's short stories."

"I guess. The point is that this guy had lost touch with reality. And you know what happens to him at the end of the story?"

"It's fiction, Cliff."

"He dies. That's what happens. Suggest anything to you?"

"We all die, Cliff."

Orville took the man's name and address. The people pulled back from the station wagon and let it pass. Halfway out of the camp, the man gunned the engine and spun the tires, sending a great cloud of choking dust into the air that floated through the camp. Orville's brother went for his pickup, but Orville stopped him.

"Come on, Eli. You're a big-city boy. Like me. There's nothing for you here. You could probably get a great settlement and go back to Toronto and live like a king."

"Nothing for me there."

"Nothing for you here, either," said Cliff. "One of these days we're going to open the flood gates and that water is going to pour down the channels and this house is going to turn into an ark."

"This is my home."

"Hell, what this is is a pile of logs in the middle of a spillway. That's what it is."

The film was blank. The people at the photo store told Leroy that it had never been used. Orville wrote the man, but the letter came back a month later marked "Unable to deliver, no such address." Leroy had copied down the man's license number. He called the Royal Canadian Mounted Police and explained what had happened. There was little they could do about it, they said. The man hadn't broken any laws.

Eli stretched and pushed his glasses back up his nose. "When I figure it out, I'll let you know."

Cliff stood and leaned over the railing. The water had receded back into the channel. "Time for me to get back. You need anything?"

"Nope. Probably go into town the next day or so." Eli walked with Cliff to the edge of the water. "What happens when it breaks?"

"The dam?"

"What happens when it breaks? You can't hold the water back forever."

Cliff jammed his walking stick into the gray-green water. "It's not going to break, Eli. Oh, it'll crack, and it'll leak. But it won't break. Just think of the dam as part of the natural landscape."

"Just thought I'd ask."

Eli watched Cliff work his way into the stream. As he climbed out on the opposite bank, Cliff turned and raised his stick over his head. Eli could see the man's mouth open and close in a shout, but all the sound was snatched up by the wind and drowned in the rushing water.

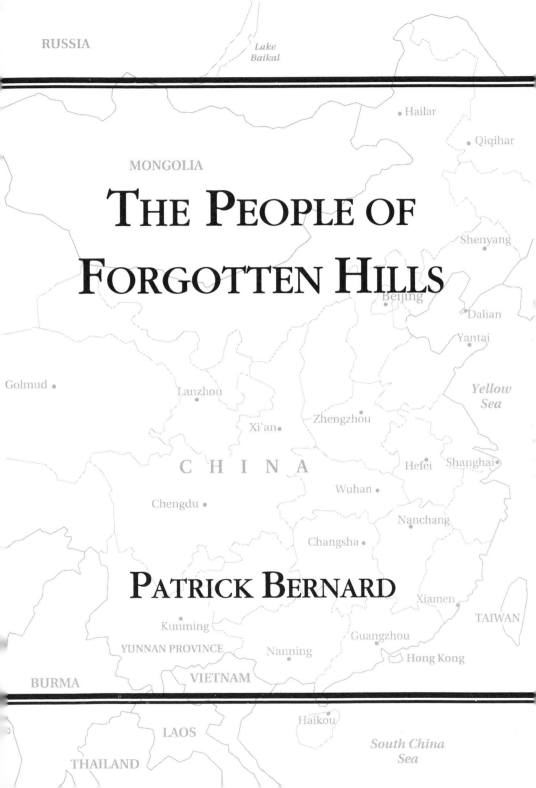

THE PEOPLE OF
FORGOTTEN HILLS

PATRICK BERNARD

P atrick Bernard was born in France. He is an ethnographer and specialist in cultural and oral traditions. The founder of ANAKO Publishing, which publishes books and materials devoted to indigenous peoples worldwide, he also established the International Commission for the Rights of Ethnic Minorities and Aboriginal Peoples, or I.C.R.A.

Mr. Bernard has traveled throughout Papua New Guinea, India, Africa, Southeast Asia, and North and South America, living among and studying indigenous peoples. Through his films and books he attempts to focus attention on the dignity of these peoples and the urgency of their plight. He is the author of several books and has produced the award-winning films "La Vallée des Hommes sans Terre" and "Mondes Secrets d'Asie." He is also a television director and a lecturer.

Mr. Bernard lives in Xonrupt-Longemer, France. The following selection is adapted from the book *Yunnan-Guizhou: Couleurs Tribales de Chine,* coauthored by Patrick Bernard and Michel Huteau.

In the distant mountains of Central Asia, where southern China, Burma, Laos, and Thailand meet, an agricultural people continue to respect the traditions and teachings of their ancestors in spite of outside influences. We met the Akha in the mountains of south Yunnan, China, and in nearby northern Thailand. Their language is a branch of the Tibetan-Burmese Yi family.

The Akha do not have a written history. All their knowledge is contained in thousands of poetic verses that have been passed from mouth to ear over generations. Their history is, in fact, a path of endless wandering.

One might expect that, like other minority groups of this region, the Akha are originally from the Tibetan plateau. However, they claim to come from farther north and to have been driven by the Chinese and Mongols to the southernmost province of China, Yunnan, where many reside today. They remained there for 2,000 years. Then, in the middle of the nineteenth century, numerous Akhas traveled west into Burma. Others migrated east toward Laos and Vietnam. Much later, during the 1960s, many Akhas fled from Laos and its totalitarian system. Almost simultaneously, entire communities left China to escape the Cultural Revolution, a period during which the authorities tried to make minorities conform and forbade the practice of their religious and philosophical beliefs. They traveled south and took refuge in the mountains of northern Thailand. Today, about 23,000 Akhas live in Thailand.

Many among them, notably those living on the peripheries of major Thai cities like Chiang Mai, are employed by travel agencies, trekkers, and drug traffickers. However, the Akha, fierce protectors of tradition, try to remain independent of the Thai population and other neighboring peoples.

From the very beginning, the Akha avoided the danger of insufficient harvests by regularly transporting their villages toward new horizons of fertile land. When the population of a village became too large or when its fields were exhausted, they could move the village to another slope, another mountain. But this seminomadic life-style and system of itinerant agriculture cannot survive long. In Thailand, competition for land is increasing; the Thai of the plains, themselves running short of cultivable land, are beginning to encroach on the mountain slopes. Regulations imposed by Chinese authorities on the province of Yunnan and other frontier regions also restrict the movement of the Akha. Faced with the impossibility of emigrating, the mountain tribes are in the process of exhausting their natural resources and land.

Climbing the muddy mountain slopes during the rainy season is not easy, but the difficulties are outweighed by the beauty of the surrounding countryside. A large Akha village opens before us, hidden in part by vegetation. The name of the village is Abbeh, which is also the name of its *dzoema*, or chief.

Our guide, Toy, leads us into the village through an impressive wooden gate decorated with sculptures. At the foot of it are two statues representing a man and a woman with exaggerated genital organs. We step onto a wide street bordered by superb bamboo and thatch homes. We are out of breath from the climb and receive surprised and sometimes frightened looks from the villagers. Abbeh arrives to meet us, dressed in a black tunic soberly embroidered at the neck and wide black trousers. He greets us warmly and invites us to his home, which is at the highest point of the village. Toy explains that here one never says "hello" or "goodbye"; one says "climb well," because in this hillside village one is always going up or coming down.

Two women welcome us. In addition to their smiling and charming faces, so finely drawn, their colorful clothing and elaborately decorated headdresses create the illusion of their having stepped out of another time.

Abbeh invites us to come inside and sit down. We are covered with mud and say that we wish to clean up. He summons a child, who takes us to a spring in a little wood below the village. While we are enjoying the spring, a young woman arrives to fill water containers that she has carried in a bamboo basket on her back. She stops and watches us with curiosity, without saying a word, until we have finished washing. She takes us to the path that leads back to the village, then, embarrassed, realizes that she has forgotten to fill her containers.

We have hardly returned to Abbeh's when he invites us to smoke opium, an invitation that we cannot decline without offending our host. The Akha men spend a lot of time preparing and smoking their opium pipes, conversing all the while. For the Akha, opium is an effective remedy against malaria, dysentery, and hunger cramps. In addition, it helps them to relax.

Evening comes, and we are invited to share the family meal. On the menu is rice accompanied by a very spicy sauce and bamboo shoots. Men and women prepare the meal together, but in general they eat separately. The daily activities of the women are quite distinct from those of the men.

The Akha, we learn, construct their villages on the hilltops of mountains, usually beneath a crest. The elders decide where a new village will be placed. The Akha have several techniques for ensuring that the spirits are in agreement with the selection of a site. The most common technique consists of digging a hole in a spot chosen by the elders. Into the hole they place three or four grains of uncooked rice, which they arrange with the utmost precision. The grains are then covered with a small bowl and left for several days. If, upon the elders' return, the grains of rice have not been moved, they conclude that the spirits have approved the location.

Sometimes the Akha use the egg technique. They clear about a square meter of ground and dig a deep hole in the center. Then the *dzoema* holds an egg at the height of his face and lets it fall into the hole. If the egg breaks, it signifies that the spirits approve the choice.

The first home to be built is the *dzoema*'s, with the assistance of all the men of the community. They then help to construct all the other homes.

A huge gate is built at the entrance of each village through which everyone must pass when arriving or leaving. At the foot of the gate are usually found wooden statues symbolizing male and female fertility. The gate is sacred. The Akha believe that the spirit of water has chosen the door of the gate as its domicile. On the lintel hang bamboo motifs that look like flowers, intended to entice the spirits to remain. Other sculpted figures show birds carrying off evil spirits and thus preventing them from entering the village.

The dwellings are built on pilings. The floors are made of bamboo, and the roofs are thatched. In the dwelling, a partition separates the men's room from the women's. Each room is itself divided into two areas: One, slightly elevated and covered with mats, is reserved for sleeping and relaxation. The other is devoted to family and household activities.

The village, the forest, and the hillsides are the domain of the men. The house, its immediate surroundings, and the fields are the domain of the women. If the men of a household are noticeably efficient in the cooking of meat or participate in certain domestic chores, the women then direct, lead the household, and are in charge of supplying water and wood.

121

A visitor cannot pass through the village without being invited into at least one home for a glass of water or some hot tea.

According to Akha mythology, every living thing is a descendant of Apoemiyeh, the spirit of life. For centuries, the oral tradition of the Akha has linked each generation to the next and taught respect for the spirit of beings and things.

Each adult male is expected to be able to recount the genealogy of his paternal ancestors through at least the sixtieth generation. This is made easier by the fact that, according to custom, the last syllable of the father's name becomes the first syllable of the son's name. When two members of an Akha clan wish to know their exact family relationship, they repeat the names of their male forebears until they find a common ancestor.

This practice is particularly useful when determining whether a young couple may marry or not. The proposed bride and groom must compare the lineage of at least twenty-seven generations on their paternal sides. If they come across a common ancestor before the twenty-seventh generation, they cannot be married, for they would be considered practically brother and sister.

An Akha considers himself an umbilical cord or deed of union between his ancestors and his descendants. For this reason, an altar is set up in each home for offerings to the spirits of the ancestors. This altar usually hangs on a wall in the area reserved for women or is attached to a roof support near the center post. The offerings are left at the altar so that the spirits of the most recent ancestors will protect and nourish the family by allowing them to harvest sufficient rice and by bringing them luck and good health.

The Akha attach great importance to the spirits of their ancestors. They believe that certain spirits are malevolent and can send them illnesses. The shaman must identify the spirit involved before using his supernatural powers to heal. The Akha also believe in guardian spirits of the family, protector spirits of the village.

For the Akha, rice is much more than food, it is a symbol of life.

An Akha legend illustrates the significance placed on a grain of rice. A widow and her thirteen-year-old daughter were in the habit of going each day to the steep banks of a nearby river to pick wild squash and roots. One day the girl disappeared. Her mother looked for her ceaselessly day after day but was unable to find her. Years later, the mother returned to the same spot to gather some of the gifts of nature. Hearing her daughter's voice calling from the waters, she plunged into the river and found her daughter in the depths of the wild waters. She had married the dragon lord, master of these waters. The mother remained a few moments in their company. The dragon lord, her son-in-law, offered her a few grains of miraculous rice wrapped in a leaf and a hollow reed. He told her that if she planted the grains of rice in a field near the village, she and her people would always have enough to eat and drink.

She planted the rice, and a few months later the harvest was so plentiful that she could not carry it all home. She returned to her son-in-law, the dragon lord, to ask his advice. He answered her in these words, "If there is too much rice, stand in the middle of your field and whistle three times; next, clap your hands three times." Thus it was done. The quantity of rice diminished, and in the space of a day she was easily able to bring back all that remained.

In memory of this legend, the Akha still use the leaf and bamboo container for the grains of rice at the time of their ritual offerings to the spirits. In addition, while they work in their fields, they are very careful never to whistle or clap their hands, lest the dragon lord believe they have more rice than they need and reduce their yield.

Before planting rice paddies, the Akha always consult the soothsayers and wait for a celestial sign to assure them of the right placement. If the omens are favorable, the peasant can clear his land.

The Akha cultivate their fields of rice, sarasin, or corn by clearing and burning the weeds on the steep flanks of the mountains that surround their villages. Once a field has been cleared, the elders determine the day on which it and all the adjoining fields will be burned. They are careful about the choice of day. If the fields are burned on the day of the monkey, they run the risk of having a fire that jumps in all directions, burning all in its path. If it is the day of the pig, the fire will nose about the soil like the snout of a pig.

A few days after planting the village fields, the Akha present offerings to the spirits of their ancestors. Then the priest of the village carries the purified seeds and deposits them in nine hallowed holes on a little altar covered in thatch, which will serve as a refuge for the soul of the rice during its growth.

At harvest time, the priest collects three clusters of the rice sown in the nine holes and leaves them on the ancestral altar of his family. Three other clusters are deposited as an offering on an altar set up in the field. The rest of the rice from the nine holes is taken to the village to be consumed during an offering ceremony. Only after this will the families of the village begin the harvest.

This afternoon several men are preparing to leave for the fields with packhorses to collect the harvest. Others remain in the village to weave baskets, repair walls and roofs ruined by rain, or tan the hides of freshly killed game.

We accompany Abbeh's wife, Abeu, and her son to the fields. All afternoon they will pick, clean, and sort peanuts. We take a few photographs. From time to time, Abeu brings us a handful of fresh peanuts that she has carefully shelled for us.

Soon, in this same field, Abeu and the others will sow poppies, which will bloom next February. After flowering, the petals will fall and leave the egg-shaped capsule containing the precious latex, which will become extract of opium.

The cultivation of poppies by the Akha is encouraged by drug traffickers. Unfortunately, the economic benefit of such cultivation is becoming indispensable to the Akhas' survival.

Today, in the Kunming hotel where we prepare to head off toward the neighboring region of Guizhou, I long for our friends from Abbeh's village, these men and women who invoke the lords of the land and water, who as they describe the springtime say, "It is the season when the dead seeds come back to life." I will never forget the songs of Abeu on her way to the spring to get water, or the songs of the young people in the evenings: "I love the sound of your voice, come back so that I can hear it again."

Translated from the French
by Jeanne Strazzabosco

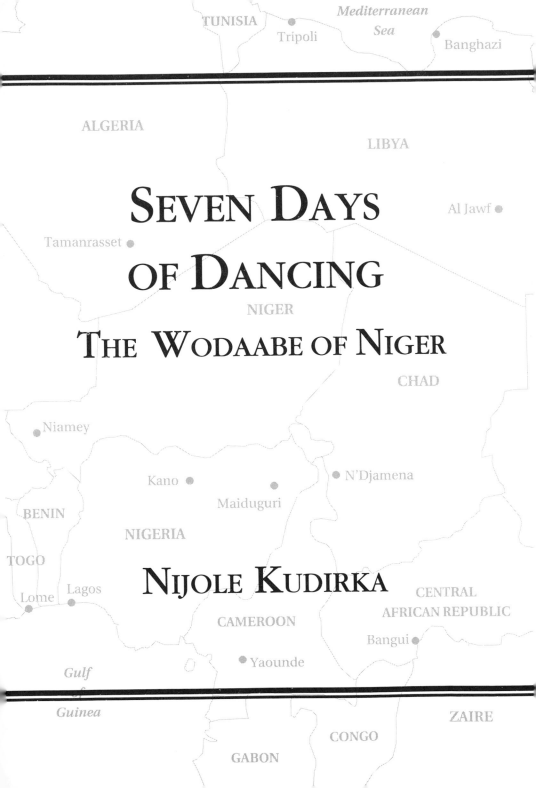

SEVEN DAYS
OF DANCING
THE WODAABE OF NIGER

NIJOLE KUDIRKA

Nijole Kudirka was born in Shakiai, Lithuania. She holds a Ph.D. in psychology from Yale University and has been in private practice for eighteen years. She also studied photography in New York City at the School of Visual Arts and the International Center of Photography.

Dr. Kudirka's work has been exhibited in New York City at the 55 Mercer Street Gallery, the National Arts Club, and, most recently, in Lithuania at the National Photo Gallery. She has published photographic essays in *Ford Times*, the *Chicago Tribune, Olympus Vision Age,* and various Lithuanian journals.

Dr. Kudirka takes a special interest in the influence of social and cultural forces on the development of individuals. She has traveled and photographed extensively in Africa, Asia, Europe, Oceania, and South America. Dr. Kudirka lives in New York City.

The Wodaabe of Niger are one of the few surviving nomadic peoples in the world. These tall (some up to seven feet), handsome herdsman live as they have for centuries, moving their herds across the parched landscape of sub-Saharan Africa. There are several lineages of Wodaabe, each clan living separately. They depend chiefly on their herds of cattle for sustenance, but they also own sheep, goats, donkeys, and camels. For other goods they are wholly dependent on trade for cattle in the marketplace. They are under constant pressure to find water and fresh pasture for their animals, and they move with their herds to adapt to the shifting weather and environmental conditions. They can break camp in less than an hour, leaving no trace of their presence, carrying their "portable houses" and all their belongings in a neat efficient pack that is loaded onto a camel or other animal. In this desert landscape, scarcely any rain falls for nine months of the year. Ponds dry up, pastures disappear, and water is hard to find. The days are extremely hot, and the nights at times are freezing cold. During the other three months of the year the rains return, the ponds are refilled, grass grows, and the cattle get fat. Then the drought begins again.

The Wodaabe adapt remarkably well to this harsh environment, making an elegant pattern of their precarious way of life. Terribly vulnerable to significant climatic changes, they suffered famine and many deaths during the great drought in 1986. The return of the rains in 1988 made life better, but their survival remains precarious.

The climax of the year for the Wodaabe is the great celebration that comes at the end of the rainy season. A Wodaabe clan invites a guest clan to join them for this celebration. Its center and focus is the Geerewol, a week-long dance performed by the handsomest young men that also serves as a beauty contest. Making up their faces is the men's most important preparation for the dance. The physical aspects they enhance are the whites of their eyes, the whiteness of their teeth, and the straightness of the nose. The projection of charisma and charm is also very important. The males compete against one another, presenting themselves to the women to be judged. The winners are selected by the three most beautiful young women. The dance is performed every afternoon and night for seven days. The man deemed most beautiful can spend the night with one of the women who selected him.

Camel driver.

Portable Wodaabe house, bundled for transport.

Wodaabe woman.

Wodaabe woman.

Wodaabe men competing at the Geerewol.

Portraits of competitors at the Geerewol.

THEY TOOK AWAY OUR RIVER

BAHER KAMAL

Baher Kamal is an Egyptian journalist affiliated with the Inter Press Service Third World News Agency, an agency specializing in coverage of Third World nations by reporters from those nations. Mr. Kamal interviewed a number of Nubian inhabitants living near the Nile River and prepared a composite report based on those interviews.

The following selection is an excerpt from the forthcoming book *Story Earth*, edited by the Inter Press Service, to be published in April 1993 by Mercury House.

For the Nubians the Nile has always been the beginning and end of all things. According to Nubian mythology, the world was born of the chaos that resulted from the dramatic arrival of the first waters of the Nile river.

On the basis of this concept the Nubians developed the idea of a spiritual relationship with the Universe, creating a cult around each of the four fundamental elements: *num* (water), *geb* (earth), *shu* (air), and *atum* or, much later, *ra*, which represented the sun and, by extension, fire.

This view was shared by the Nubian and Egyptian peoples who, in the predynastic era, that is, before 3200 B.C., not only were one homogeneous people but, above all, shared a common culture. But by the middle of the third millennium B.C., Nubians and Egyptians had begun to drift apart in customs and traditions.

According to some scholars, Nubian territory comprised one third of present-day Egypt, the whole of Sudan, and parts of Ethiopia, always flanking both banks of the Nile. In a word, Nubian culture centered almost exclusively on the Nile, and the annual rise in the level of its water was a regular source of joy and fear.

Joy, because the lime carried in its waters was a natural fertilizer for the soil and helped ensure the growth of abundant crops. Fear, because on occasion the rise in the level of the river was such that land and houses were flooded. That is why Nubians developed the tradition of making offerings to the Nile in the form of baskets of food, seeds, and beautiful handmade objects.

This culture and way of life survived the military campaigns mounted by the Egyptians against Nubian lands starting around 2000 B.C., and the annexation of a sizable portion of the country, stretching from Edfu to northern Sudan. Nubia eventually came to govern Egypt during the 25th Dynasty, with five Nubian Pharaohs overseeing the destiny of the region in the period 747–656 B.C.

Although the world witnessed a series of major historical developments over the next several centuries, none created deep change in the life of the Nubian people. In the 7th century A.D. the Roman leadership in Egypt obliged the Nubians to adopt Christianity. The new forms of worship did not radically replace traditional beliefs or religious rituals, which continued to be performed in synchronicity with the behavior of the Nile.

Five centuries ago, the Nubian people were subjected to invasion by the Ottoman Turks and the imposition of Islam as the official religion. Even then, families that converted to Islam continued their traditional religious ceremonies and rituals in a surprising mix of the ancient, Christian, and Moslem beliefs.

Meanwhile, the Nile remained constant. The soil bathed by its water provided the Nubians with food. The land straddling both banks of the river supplied the material to build houses and form villages. Thus, life continued without significant change through the start of the 20th century, up to the moment when the first dam was built at Aswan, Egypt, in 1902 to control the flow of the Nile and ensure adequate supplies of water throughout most of the year.

Then the Nubians suffered what could be called their first forced mass migration. With the building of the Aswan Dam, Nubians lost one third of their land.

Work carried out in 1912 and 1933 to increase the height of the dam brought about further displacement and the loss of an additional third of the land.

However, the most profound change occurred in the 1960s with the construction of the Aswan High Dam and Nasser Lake. The dam is a mass of concrete and iron measuring some 43 million cubic meters in volume. Nasser Lake, with a surface area of 225 square kilometers, is Africa's largest artificial reservoir and one of the largest in the world.

When construction was proposed, the voice of alarm rang in all four corners of the world: This herculean feat of modern engineering would bury forever a host of architectural masterpieces, witnesses to the glory of the Egypt of the Pharaohs, under the waters of an artificial lake. To rescue magnificent archeological monuments such as the Abu Simbel temples, a worldwide alliance was created.

Despite the effort, little was said about the fate facing the Nubians, whose houses were destined to disappear forever under the waters of the lake. The governments of Egypt and Sudan did draw up plans to relocate the displaced Nubians (for the dam and the lake also affected the northern part of the neighboring country). Thirty years later, houses and plots of land have still not been assigned to some of those Nubians displaced earlier.

But more important, and this is the crux of the issue, direct contact with the Nile was definitively altered. It was a hard blow to Nubian culture and traditions.

Today, in the new houses, water arrives through pipes. The region where most of the displaced people resettled in Egypt, Kom Ombo, is more that 200 kilometers from former settlements. It does not offer the same living conditions that Nubians used to have. Some houses are built at the very edge of the desert, ten kilometers from the river. The soil is arid and infertile.

Farmers and fisherfolk had no choice but to move to the cities to find work, along with many other Nubian men and women, as house servants, waiters, and porters. Not even the agricultural rehabilitation projects established for the land beside the artificial lake or concessions set up for Nubian fisherfolk have worked properly, often because of bureaucratic red tape.

The new houses are much smaller than those Nubians were used to, which were much more than simple dwellings: They allowed for a spacious family nucleus.

As one example of ancient traditions, the family of a

recently married young woman opened up their home to her new husband for a period that could last up to two years. This tradition fulfilled two functions: It accustomed the husband to the ways of the wife's family, and it helped the husband save money to build a house nearby. But this custom is no longer possible because the smaller houses lack the extra space for a married couple.

In Egypt alone Nubians were previously spread throughout some 600 villages; today, Nubian villages number just 43. In Sudan, the same phenomenon occurred, with the additional problem that the 50,000 people affected were transferred to Khashm el-Girba, some 600 kilometers away from their ancestral lands.

The agricultural land that has been assigned to the Nubian people in the new settlements lacks quality, is often insufficient, and much of it is far from living areas. And Nubians have been forced to adopt different forms of agriculture, like growing sugarcane.

The water rationed to Nubians for irrigation no longer contains lime, meaning that chemical fertilizers now have to be used. This is not good for the soil, the crops, or the health of the people, who often do not know how to use these new fertilizers.

There has been a heavy migration of men. This is the result of the change in patterns of traditional sources of survival, which has meant that Nubian men have acquired new urban customs and ways, many of them Western, and that they have married non-Nubian women. This has helped lead to the disintegration of the nuclear family— one of the pillars of Nubian culture, where one's family was the entire village.

The worldwide campaign to save the monuments of the land of the Nubians has given birth to mass tourism, which in turn has either attracted or obliged young people to move into the service sector, at the expense of agriculture or fishing. The contact with foreigners has also led to the superimposition of Western customs onto Nubian traditions.

The elders believe that the drought that has affected the Nile region for the last nine years is a direct result of the construction, which changed the flow and life of the river. In this sense, what some technical experts say is true: With the construction of the High Dam, the Nile was broken off at Aswan. From there to its mouth in the Mediterranean, the Nile has been transformed into a virtual canal.

One of the most serious problems was the loss of the lime that fertilized the soil naturally. Now, it is all blocked behind the dam.

But the lime was useful for more than fertilizing the soil. Many Nubians worked in the almost 7,000 small factories that used lime to create building material. Now they are unemployed, twenty years after being promised that a new factory would be built.

Further, the loss of lime has created problems for sardine fisherman, because the once abundant sardines fed on lime. While it is true that, over time, fish stocks have increased thanks to Nasser Lake, it is also true that those who lived from sardine fishing and small family industries have suffered a major economic and social setback.

Finally, the lack of lime has led to substantial soil erosion, not only along the banks of the Nile. The delta lands to the north of Egypt are more exposed to the waters of the Mediterranean because the lime formed a sort of barrier as well as a source of natural fertility.

The problems do not end here. With the huge quantity of liquid amassed in the lake, and the lack of adequate drainage systems, the level of subterranean water has risen dramatically and dangerously.

Monuments are directly affected by these developments because the underground water level has risen to the depth of their foundations. For example, at the Temple of Karnak, in Luxor, the foundations have suffered water damage. The interior of the Temple of Nefertiti is more affected by moisture than is the exterior. The Sphinx runs the same risk.

This is not to suggest that the High Dam and the reservoir have not brought benefits, that no attempt has been made to solve many of the concomitant problems, or that Nubians oppose the development of Egypt. But the price the Nubian people have paid and continue to pay is very high. Above all else, the Nubians have lost their identity.

Nubians are doing what they can to safeguard their traditions. To help maintain contact among the million Nubians estimated to live in Egypt (another million live in Sudan), forty-three associations have been created.

The associations are meeting places for Nubians, places where they celebrate weddings in those cases—increasingly frequent—when they cannot do so in their villages; communal vigils are organized upon the death of a Nubian by his people; collections are made to help the neediest; news is exchanged; songs are sung, and folklore evenings are held. And there the people can speak their own dialects. This is of extreme importance for the conservation of the Nubian languages, no longer written but still spoken.

The effort is to revive some of the traditions of their ancestors, even if Nubians live far from the lands of those ancestors—lands that are now irreversibly under water—and far from their families, who have been torn apart.

That is the price that the Nubian people—who have given much to Egypt, who developed their own formidable culture, who once knew abundant harvests and practiced fishing but now serve as waiters in the big cities—have had to pay for a modern technology that has tried to domesticate the Nile, their Nile, and to generate electric energy to ensure that, among others, the TV set of today can show never-ending hours of foreign films.

Translated from the Dutch
by Scott Rollins

THE MASQUERADE DANCERS OF HAVANA

HELIO OROVIO AND HECTOR DELGADO PÉREZ

Helio Orovio was born in Havana, Cuba, in 1938. He is a writer, poet, and musicologist. Mr. Orovio has written numerous articles and essays that have been published in Cuban journals as well as abroad. He is a member of the Music Association of the Union of Artists and Writers of Cuba (UNEAC). He is the author of *Diccionario de la Musica Cubana* and editor of an anthology on the *bolero* in Latin America.

Hector Delgado Pérez was born in Havana, Cuba. He is one of Cuba's premier photographers. Since 1982, he has been the official photographer of the UNEAC.

Mr. Delgado's work has been exhibited in Canada, Mexico, and the United States, and his photographs have appeared in newspapers and journals in Latin America and Eastern Europe. He has received awards for his photography in Cuba, Bulgaria, and Russia and from the World Health Organization.

Hector Delgado Pérez

The following selection is adapted from their forthcoming book, edited by Margarite Fernández Olmos, *El Carnival de La Habana: Un Ballet Afrocubano,* to be published by Editorial Limusa, Mexico.

T he *comparsas* or masquerade dancers of Havana are indisputably the nucleus from which the rich tradition of the Cuban carnival developed. These societies of dancers date from the Spanish colonial period (1512-1898). They originated among the Afrocuban societies or *cabildos* that used to go into the streets on Epiphany, grouped by ethnic nations—the Congolese, the Lucumí or Yoruba of present-day Nigeria, the Mandinga of Guinea, the Carabalí of Calabar, the Arará of Dahomey—and make their way through the city to the palace of the Captain General. There they would present greetings to the colonial authorities and receive New Year's gifts. This was the only day that the slave had for singing, beating his drums, and dancing, forgetting for a few hours his lowly condition in a society dominated by Spaniards and economically based on African slave labor. Even the slave's Sunday festivities were limited to the sugar-mill towns. Epiphany was the one day when he could express joy and maintain the basic elements of his culture, defending them against the eagerness of the ruling class to exterminate them. Documents exist dating from 1823 in which Governor Dionisio Vives authorized these African organizations to pass through the city streets.

Epiphany, January 6, was the day on which the Spaniards exchanged gifts in celebration of the Christmas season and likewise the one true holiday that they gave to their slaves. It is ironic, then, that only on that Christian religious holiday were the slaves fully able to celebrate their traditional religion.

Yoruba spirituality, widespread then as now in Cuba, is founded on belief in the existence of several *orichas* or deities. Some people call them gods, but the concept of the Greek god has nothing to do with this cosmogony. They are

deities, beings in whom the African believes. Transplanted to Cuba, the belief was adapted into a Cuban spirituality.

For Afrocubans, their music, song, and dance were not merely artistic performance. They were radical, deeply rooted in their African cultural beginnings. For them, music and dance found their source in the earth; they were magical expressions directly related to their system of beliefs. People of Yoruba, Lucumí, Carabalí, or Arará origins had a rich mythology that was expressed in music, songs, dance, dress, body language.

One of the Afrocuban deities, Elegguá, guards the crossroads; he is a spy and a messenger for the other *orichas*. Ochún is the deity of wit, laughter, celebration, congeniality. Because of her symbolic link with river water, river banks are sites of ceremonies held in her honor. Yemayá is a graver, more profound being. She is the deity of the seas, of salt water, and her realm is in the depths of the sea. Changó, the King of Oyó, is a warrior deity of virility, strength, and fortitude. Obatalá is a deity of wisdom, peace, tranquility, balance. Oggún is the deity of metals and of the forge.

But just as the imposition of Spanish culture and the attempt to quash African culture limited the Africans' musical and dance expression to one day a year, it also forced them more generally to disguise their religious practices. They did so by making their deities syncretic with saints of the Roman Catholic religion, associating their forbidden deities with the acceptable foreign saints. However, this syncretism, or fusion, was rather superficial: To say that Yemayá is the Virgin of Regla, that Ochún is the Virgin of Caridad del Cobre, or that Changó is Saint Barbara would reflect a shallow understanding of the phenomenon. A deeper consideration reveals that for the Cubans of African ancestry the gods of their land continued to be distinct from the saints revered by the Spanish colonialists. African spirituality was therefore masked by apparent worship of Catholic saints. The concealment was a means of realizing another objective:

151

to mock prohibitions against practice of their authentic worship. For their masters they appeared to worship the Virgin Mary and other saints; in their hearts, they worshipped Yemayá, Ochún, Changó, Oggún, Obatalá. This combination of circumstances produced the religion called *santería*.

Further, in the African culture brought to Cuba by the slaves, music constituted a system of symbols. Music moved one's inner fiber and transported one toward one's ancestors. When Afrocubans danced, they formed a bond with their ancestors; when they sang, they paid homage to their forebears; when they beat a drum, they sent a message—for the Africans, the drum spoke. Communication was oral in Africa. Songs, drumbeats, dances were their system of expression. The function of the drums, the iron devices, the conch whistles, the rattles, the primitive trumpets made of bones and shells, was communication. What a European expressed by written symbols, an African transmitted by sound produced by the voice or by percussion instruments.

Thus the celebration by the Afrocuban societies on Epiphany was a profound affirmation of traditional beliefs and practices.

In the early colonial days, on Epiphany, the Afrocuban societies typically wore garments, ornaments, and masks native to Africa. Gradually they began to include clothing and objects once owned by their masters, items received as gifts or bought for a few coins in small shops. In the second half of the nineteenth century, these castoff clothes replaced the colorful African costumes entirely. The cutaway coat, the bowler hat, the elegant dresses imitating those of the "mistresses" took the place of the short, blue-striped shirts, the red percale trousers, and the plumed hats of the Congolese and the Lucumí; the blue silk turbans typical of the Mandinga; the straw fringes worn at the waist, the ornately decorated mesh shirts, the top hats, and the bells of the Abakuá imps—the so-called Ñáñigos, members of a

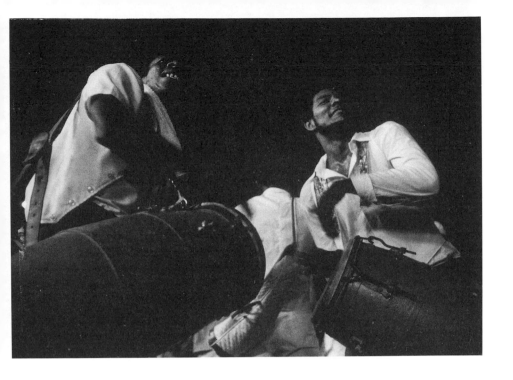

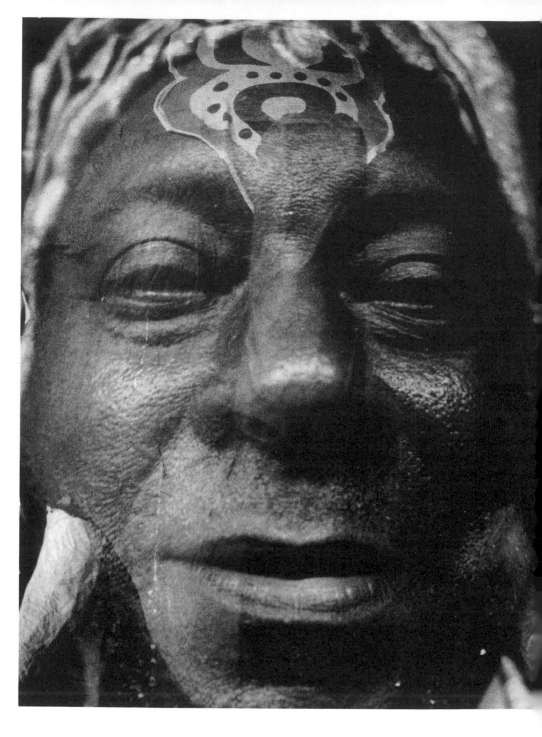

secret society begun in the Nigerian Calabar and developed in Cuba. Fusion of cultures also occurred in the musical sphere. The Cuban conga*, of African origin in its basic structure, kept absorbing elements arising from the white stratum of society, of European ancestry, amalgamating or "transculturing" them, as Cuban ethnographer Fernando Ortiz would say.

The result of this interaction was what one might expect. During the nineteenth century and even in the first years of the twentieth century, two carnivals were held in Havana. One, imposed by the dominant white class, was held just before Lent; the other, germinated in the soil of the common people, was held on Epiphany. The "white" or Spanish carnival took place during the three days preceding Ash Wednesday. There were drives in open two-wheeled carts, later replaced by elegant state coaches. As the "ladies" and "gentlemen" drove along, they strewed flowers, precursors of today's confetti and paper streamers. After the drives, cotillions, waltzes, minuets, and rigadoons resounded in the celebrated balls held in the Tacón Theater.

Toward the end of the nineteenth century, the Afrocuban celebration of Epiphany was outlawed, and the two carnivals took place together in March. State coaches and regular carriages were juxtaposed with the marvelous *comparsas*, dancing societies that had evolved from the Afrocuban societies. Each *comparsa* was known for its unique costumes, songs, and choreography, dancing as a group to the accompaniment of drums and other Afrocuban instruments. Among them were the outstanding La culebra (The Snake), El pájaro lindo (The Pretty Bird), and El gavilán (The Sparrow Hawk).

Then, during the so-called Bloody Carnival of 1894, a violent quarrel erupted among rival factions of the

---

*conga—Cuban dance performed by a group following a leader in a single line.

Abakuá. This gave colonial authorities an excuse to order suspension of carnival entertainments in the following year when the War of Independence began anew under the leadership of José Martí. In 1898, after the civil strife had ended and Spain had lost the Spanish-American War to the United States, thus forfeiting all claim to Cuba, the *comparsas* again went into the streets of the newly independent nation in all their colorful character, only to be curtailed once more in 1908 for political reasons. Collective popular gatherings of any type were viewed with suspicion by the established authorities who regarded them as a potential threat to order.

Examining the list of *comparsas* participating prior to 1908, one sees the diversity of themes and of productions that had arisen from the folkloric quarters of Havana: Los chinos buenos (The Good Chinese), Los hijos de Chávez (Chávez's Children), Los marinos de Regla (Regla's Seamen), Los moros rosados (The Rose-Colored Moors), Los guajiros del jiquí (The Rustics from Jiquí), Los jóvenes del jardín (The Garden Youths), Los Cuban Minstrels (in imitation of the song and dance groups from the Southern United States), and the legendary El alacrán (The Scorpion), which still parades in Cuba's carnivals. Los guajiros del jiquí, according to José Luciano Franco, were a group of white people and renegade mulattos who intoned only stanzas of ten eight-syllable lines called *décimas*. They kept time by beating their feet on the ground, accompanied by guitars and bandores, completely rejecting the traditional African drums.

Five years later, in 1913, there was consideration of reauthorizing the *comparsas*, under police guard, without drums or other Afrocuban instruments, and without their typical dances; in other words, there was thought of allowing *comparsas* without the essential elements of the *comparsa*. The idea led, however, to no action. They did reappear, timidly, in 1927, but immediately the regime of

Gerardo Machado suppressed them, fearing any kind of public gathering. Not until 1937 did they reemerge, thanks to the efforts of Fernando Ortiz, José Luciano Franco, Nicolás Guillén, and other intellectuals and artists concerned about rescuing folkloric values of Cuban culture. In that year the *comparsas* paraded through the Paseo del Prado with their big lanterns, their carefully designed dances, their choral singing, their costumes, and their music.

After the Revolution in 1959, some of the traditional *comparsas* continued to perform in the first carnivals of the 1960s. But the new historical, political, and social scene generated by the revolutionary process was reflected in changes in the nature of the carnival, and generally speaking, *comparsas* faded from the Cuban cultural scene until the end of the 1970s. At that time, visible efforts to rescue the traditional dance groups of the carnival of Havana began. Research done for the Ministry of Culture's *Atlas of Popular Culture*, and an immense body of work done by folklorists and other specialists slowly recreated and reconstructed these all but vanished institutions.

For instance, the *comparsa* called Los guaracheros (The Cloggers), from Regla, was founded thirty years ago. Rehearsals for the legendary El alacrán continue as always in the historic premises on El Salvador Street, and it maintains its classic legend that originated in the nineteenth-century sugar mill. The Scorpion presents the actions of cane-cutters, overseers, and other characters.

The district of Jesús María boasts the *comparsa* Las jardineras (The Gardeners), a very beautiful group. The women are dressed in brightly colored skirts, blouses, and kerchiefs, and the men wear broadly contrasting fabrics, with kerchiefs at the waist and at the neck. The women carry a basket filled with flowers.

The Belén neighborhood restored Los dandys (The Dandies), the famous *comparsa* founded in 1937. It was in

Belén, near the wharves, that the rumba was first danced in Havana, and it has always been a reservoir of Afrocuban music. The costumes of the group are quite elegant: white jacket, black tie, bowler, and walking stick for the men, and long, dark dress for the women.

Las boyeras (The Cowherds), established in 1937, have continued to take part in the carnival parades, with their Afrocuban costumes imitating the fritter vendors who used to fill the city streets. The central figure is their singer, called a *clarina* (clarion), who intones prayers to the Yoruban deities.

The Chinese district of downtown Havana performs its Danza del León (Lion Dance), a part of Havana's carnival since the 1940s.

A "roving ballet" is poet Alejo Carpentier's description of a *comparsa*. His definition is quite fitting, because it is obvious that the dancers fit into an enormous tableau. It goes along dancing its productions, its themes, its choreographies, and its music to the rhythm of the conga. The conga, of all Cuban dances, is the one that best expresses the Cuban identity.

"The *comparsas*," Alberto Arredondo wrote three decades ago, "with their color, their distinctive zest, their need to form clusters, their requirement of uniformity, their demand for collective dancing and their infectious conga steps—which are a thousand short steps rooted in one and the same emotion—have continuously demonstrated that they constitute the national dance of Cuba. And, a curious detail: They constitute the most artistic, the most elegant, the most joyful and, at the same time, the most moral of all Cuban dances. It's the only Cuban dance that is not based, sensually, on the conquest of the female! The *comparsas*, unending dance of tireless bodies, of mouths never weary of laughing, of legs never tired of dancing!"

Translated from the Spanish
by Mary Eloise Herbert and Rafael Ocasio

Glossary

abhorrent—causing disgust

amalgamate—to combine or blend

buffet—to beat back as by repeated blows

calabash—the dried, hollow shell of a gourd or calabash used as a bowl or cup

cataclysm—violent upheaval

continence—self restraint

cosmogony—the study of the origin of the universe

culinary—of the kitchen or cooking

diaspora—any scattering of people with a common origin, background, beliefs

diffuse—to spread out or disperse

embellish—to decorate or improve by adding detail

Epiphany—in many Christian churches, a festival held January sixth, commemorating the revealing of Jesus as the Christ to the Gentiles in the persons of the Magi

euphoria—a feeling of vigor, well-being, or high spirits

foray—a sudden attack in order to seize or steal things

genocide—a program of action intended to destroy a whole national or ethnic group

goashore—cooking implement

he tangi ki te po—weeping in the dark

homogeneous—the same in structure, quality; similar or identical

insatiable—constantly wanting more; unable to be satisfied or appeased

insurrection—a rising up against established authority; rebellion, revolt

jubilant—joyful and triumphant

juxtapose—to put side by side

kaihaukai—seasonal festival

kareko—transliteration for calico

Kati Tio—the narrator's tribe

kauta—detached building subordinate to a house

keen—to wail or lament

kotuku—white heron

maremare—disease

maro—sleeveless article of clothing

monopoly—exclusive possession or control of something

nomad—member of a people having no permanent home, moving about constantly in search of food and pasture

ostensible—evident

paradigm—a pattern, example, or model

parochialism—excessive narrowness of interests or views

permeate—to pass into or through and affect every part of

poua—grandfather

precarious—uncertain, insecure

primordial—first in time; existing at or from the beginning; primitive; primeval

prolific—fruitful; abounding

proscribe—to prohibit, banish or exile

protagonist—the main character in a drama, novel, or story

pungent—producing a sharp sensation of taste or smell

quash—destroy

ramification—a derived effect, consequence, or result

rimurapa—type of plant

rivet—to fix or hold (the eyes or attention) firmly

shaman—a priest or medicine man

solidarity—complete unity

syncopate—to shift the regular accent, beginning a tone on an unaccented beat and continuing it through the next accented beat

tamait'—child

taniwha—mythical monster

taua—grandmother

totalitarian—authoritarian, autocratic, dictatorial

travesty—a distorted representation of something

viscous—cohesive and fluid in consistency

weka—type of fish

whare—house

Bibliography

Achebe, Chinua. *Hopes and Impediments*. New York: Doubleday, 1989. Nonfiction: Collection of essays and speeches by the Nigerian novelist reflecting on the present needs of his society.

———. *No Longer at Ease*. Portsmouth, NH: Heinemann Educational Books Inc., 1983. Fiction: The story of an African tragically under pressure from a changing world.

Achebe, Chinua, and Innes, C.L., eds. *Contemporary African Short Stories*. Portsmouth, NH: Heinemann Educational Books Inc., 1992. An anthology of the best new African writers from across the continent.

Al Hakim, Tawfiq. *Maze of Justice: Diary of a Country Prosecutor*. Austin: University of Texas Press, 1989. Fiction: The narrator records the investigation of a peasant's murder, weaving together experiences of peasant life vs. city life in Egypt.

Bushnaq, Inea. *Arab Folktales*. New York: Pantheon, 1989. Fiction: Collection of traditional Arab folktales.

Deloria Jr., Vine, and Lytle, Clifford M. *The Nations Within: The Past and Future of American Indian Sovereignty*. New York: Pantheon, 1984. Nonfiction: Historical account showing the complexity of Native American relations with federal and state governments.

Edgell, Zee. *Beka Lamb*. Portsmouth, NH: Heinemann Educational Books Inc., 1982. Fiction: Story, set in Belize, of a few months in the life of Beka and her family.

Erdrich, Louise. *Love Medicine*. New York: Bantam Books, 1984. Fiction: A moving saga of two Native American families.

Galeano, Eduardo. *Memory of Fire*. New York: Pantheon. Fiction: Trilogy recounting the epic history of the Americas, a Latin American view of a New World in the making.

Harner, Michael. *The Way of the Shaman*. San Francisco: Harper San Francisco, 1990. Nonfiction: An intimate and practical guide to the art of shamanic healing and the technology of the sacred.

Hove, Chenjerai. *Bones.* Portsmouth, NH: Heinemann Educational Books, 1990. Fiction: The struggle of a farm laborer in Zimbabwe on a white commercial farm.

Hudson, Mark. *Our Grandmother's Drums.* New York: Grove Weidenfeld, 1990. Nonfiction: The author recounts his experience in a Gambian village and his efforts to learn about the Mandingo women.

Hudson, Peter. *A Leaf in the Wind.* New York: Walker & Co., 1989. Nonfiction: Hiking and hitchhiking through Africa, the author finds that people can enjoy life without Western materialism and values.

Hulme, Keri. *The Bone People.* New York: Viking Penguin, 1983. Fiction: Explores the relationship between three New Zealanders, two of them Maori.

Keneally, Thomas. *Flying Hero Class.* New York: Warner Books Inc., 1991. Fiction: A plane carrying a troupe of Australian aboriginal dancers from New York to Frankfurt on the last leg of a world tour is highjacked.

King, Thomas. *Medicine River.* New York: Viking Penguin, 1990. Fiction: The narrator returns home from Toronto and opens the first Native American photography business.

Larsen, Jeanne. *Silk Road.* New York: Henry Holt & Co. Inc., 1989. Fiction: Set during the Tang Dynasty in eighteenth-century China, a slave girl searches for identity.

Maybury-Lewis, David. *Millennium: Tribal Wisdom and the Modern World.* New York: Viking, 1992. Nonfiction: Examines what we have lost in our race toward the future and what essentials we have cast aside along the way. Features photographs of several indigenous peoples.

McKnight, Reginald. *I Get on the Bus.* New York: Little, Brown & Co. Inc., 1990. Fiction: A young African American boy searches for his roots via the Peace Corps in Senegal.

Momaday, N. Scott. *House Made of Dawn*. New York: Harper & Row, 1989. Fiction: A young American Indian struggles in his two worlds, traditional and modern.

Mungoshi, Charles. *The Setting Sun and the Rolling World*. Boston: Beacon Press, 1989. Fiction: Collection of stories by the Zimbabwean author about contemporary life in his country.

Munif, Abdelrahman. *The Trench*. New York: Pantheon,1991. Fiction: The second book in a trilogy explores from different and conflicting angles the tensions in society that the oil age has created.

Oyono, Ferdinand. *Road to Europe*. Washington, DC: Three Continents Press, 1989. Fiction: An educated Cameroonian explains why he persisted in going to France.

Said, Edward. *The Question of Palestine*. New York: Vintage Books, 1980. Nonfiction: The author discusses the emergence of the modern Palestinian nation and its confrontation with Zionism and Israel.

Saitoti, Tepilit Ole. *Maasai*. New York: Harry N. Abrams, Inc., 1980. The Maasai author documents ancient legends, songs, and prayers and vividly describes the stages of life of his people.

Stoller, Paul. *Fusion of the Worlds; An Ethnography of Possession Among the Songhay of Niger*. Chicago: University of Chicago Press, 1989. Nonfiction: Through description of ceremonies of actual spirit possession, the author examines the lives of a Songhay possession troupe and the history of this phenomenon.

Thiong'o, Ngugi Wa. *Matigari*. Portsmouth, NH: Heinemann Educational Books Inc., 1987. Fiction: A man who has survived the war for independence in an unnamed country emerges from the mountains and starts making strange claims and demands.

Toer, Pramoedya Ananta. *This Earth of Mankind*. New York: William Morrow & Co. Inc., 1991. Fiction: The story of the coming of age of Minke, a young Javanese in a world of Dutch colonizers.

Vargas Llosa, Mario. *The Storyteller*. New York: Farrar, Straus & Giroux, 1989. Fiction: A Peruvian novelist dicovers that his friend has become the storyteller for an Indian jungle tribe that resists the modern world.

Vassanji, M.G. *The Gunny Sack*. Portsmouth, NH: Heinemann Educational Books Inc., 1989. Fiction: The story of an extended family's arrival and life in East Africa, and a treasury of memories and oral history of many other Asian Africans.

Walker, Alice. *Possessing the Secret of Joy*, New York: Harcourt Brace Jovanovich, 1992. Fiction: The story of a tribal African woman struggling with her people's custom of genital mutilation.

———. *The Temple of My Familiar*, New York: Harcourt Brace Jovanovich, 1989. Fiction: Characters reconnect with missing pieces of their past, from precolonial Africa to post-slavery North Carolina and modern-day San Francisco.

Index

A
Abedi, Barima Asante III, 48-58
Africa, 3-17, 45-58, 73-84, 129-130, 141-146
Afrocuban societies, 149-161
Akato, Osei Yaw, 45-58
Alberta, 103-114
Aphreh, Victor, 46-58
Arnhem Aboriginal Land Reserve, 31-41
Arredondo, Alberto, 160
Asafo, Ghana, 45-58
Aswan Dam, 141-146
Australia, 31-41

B
burial tradition, African, 3-17, 54-57
Burma, 117

C
Canada, 103-114
Carpentier, Alejo, 160
Central Asia, 103-114
Charles, Kwame, 46-58
China, 117
comparsas, 149-160
conga, 156
conquistadors, 22-23
Cortés, Hernán, 22
Cuba, 149-160
cuisine, American, 21-27
Cullen, Countee, 46
Cultural Revolution, 117
culture
    aboriginal, 31-41
    African, 3-17, 73-84
    Afrocuban, 149-161
    Nubian, 141-146

D
dam, building of, 103-114, 141-146
dance festival, 108-111, 129-130, 149-160
dingo, 32-34, 38, 41
DuBois, W.E.B., 48

E
East Indies, 24-25
Egypt, 141-146
Epiphany, 149-160

F
Franco, José, Luciano, 157, 158

G
genocide, 50-53
Ghana, 45-58

H
healer, tribal, 31-41, 87-99
Heinz Company, 24
history, oral, 73-84
Hove, Chenjerai, 73, 74-78

I
indigenous peoples, 3-17, 61-69
Indonesia, 87-99
infidelity, marital, 3-17
initiation, tribal, 34-37, 80-84

K
Karnak, Temple of, 145-146
ketchup vs. salsa, 21-27

L
land, appropriation of, 103-114
Liking, Werewere, 73, 78-84
literature, African, 73-84

M
Machado, Gerardo, 158
Maori, 61-69
Melville, Herman, 112-113
Mentawaï, 87-99
mining, 31-41
missionaries, 31-35, 57-58, 94
mythology
    Akha, 122-124
    Mentawaï, 88-93

N
Nasser Lake, 142-143
New Zealand, 61-69
Niger, 129-130
Nile River, 141-146
nomads, 129-130

O
opium, 119, 125
Ortiz, Fernando, 156, 158

R
reincarnation, 31-41
rice cultivation, 123-124
rituals, religious, 142

S

Saint George, Castle of, 50-53
salsa vs. ketchup, 21-27
santería, 152
shaman, 87-99
Slavery Abolition Act, 41
slavery, 61-69, 149-152
slave trade, 45-58
soy sauce, 23
storytelling, 74-78
Sun Dance, 108-111

T

Thailand, 117-125
theater, ritual, 80-84
tomato, 21-27
tortillas, 23
tribes
    Abakuá, 152
    African, 3-17
    Akha, 117-123
    Blackfoot, 103-114
    Carabalí, 149, 151
    Congolese, 149, 152

    Lucumí, 149,151, 152
    Mandinga, 149, 152
    Wodaabe, 129-130
    Yoruba, 149, 151
    yuln, 31-41

V

Vives, Dionisio, 149

W

whites
    in Africa, 3-17
    in Indonesia, 87-99
    and Native Americans, 103-114
    in New Zealand, 61-69
Wilberforce, William, 41
women, equality of, 3-17

Y

Youngblood, Johnny Ray, 45-58
yuln tribe, 31-41

Z

Zimbabwe, 74-78